Collected Works

by

Marc Chomel

DORRANCE PUBLISHING CO., INC.
PITTSBURGH, PENNSYLVANIA 15222

The contents of this work including, but not limited to, the accuracy of events, people, and places depicted; opinions expressed; permission to use previously published materials included; and any advice given or actions advocated are solely the responsibility of the author, who assumes all liability for said work and indemnifies the publisher against any claims stemming from publication of the work.

All Rights Reserved
Copyright © 2014 by Marc Chomel

No part of this book may be reproduced or transmitted, downloaded, distributed, reverse engineered, or stored in or introduced into any information storage and retrieval system, in any form or by any means, including photocopying and recording, whether electronic or mechanical, now known or hereinafter invented without permission in writing from the publisher.

Dorrance Publishing Co., Inc.
701 Smithfield Street
Pittsburgh, PA 15222
Visit our website at *www.dorrancebookstore.com*

ISBN: 978-1-4349-3691-2
eISBN: 978-1-4349-3611-0

Dedicated to my mother,

Dr. Luisetta Chomel

POEMS

HER

I hear the violin,
Complaining,
As we always do,
Of needing freedom,
Screeching in want,
For skin, and red lips,
Offering the taste of papaya,
Lick, touch and feel that pink dress,
Slip down around you,
A small kiss at your throat,
That bolts your neck forward,
And cements your smile into mine.

A stanza of sad lyrics stands you up,
How could I know you?
But somehow your eyes give you away,
As old friends up that dirt trail of school,

When we were ten, skirting the snakes,
In the evil ditches from which we were banned,
In that true humid air,
I sometimes hear the rattling sound of a moccasin,
In the way you walk.
A woman is a parade of vanity,
There is nothing left of the girl,
That walked with me to first grade.
I teeter now upon an old fence,
That separates hope from hell,
And dare to traipse upon the quicksand,
Of my weathered confidence,
In search of an R.S.V.P.

Delicate aromas encircle the path,
Behind your taloned feet,
Wily legs of brown march enigmatically,
To stake your space and measure,
Above all your capacity.
Martyr to brave heroine,
That stamps out all with grave delight.

I hear that L.A. is cool,
Would you like to see my work?
Joe gets the Folk Art, film, and North Dakotan folklore,
Lost on his multimedia calendar,
But occasionally dines
Where you toil,
At Shilly's Steakhouse.

Proud woman walking her straight line,
Wired for sound and the perfect catch,
Harder to get and harder to latch,
In a box of her own design.

When in your sweet perfection,
I watched you from afar,
Too afraid to touch the heat,
Of your magenta lips and black claws,
That wanted to sacrifice the good red meat,
To my Piscean pathos and romantic dreams.

For whom do you wear that skirt,
And wander swiftly in fishnet hose?
Like a diva on a mission,
Clickety clack, clickety clack,
Like a platoon set to conquer,
Something.

I remember a smile through auburn curls,
A wit that scathed but sympathized,
On a couch in an upstairs bar,
Where Mahler played, the wine was good,
And your lips kissed me first,
Before I kissed them.

I remember that place in Ios,
Where I resurrected you,
Watching those moonlit Odyssean seas,
I loved you then,
But you said I must be drunk.

I love that warm and silky place,
That undulates in ecstasy,
Like a throttle of good company,
Does it mean you love me?
Or is this simply a spinning stretch,
Of good exercise?

Chlorox well your floors and ideas.
Wave away my smoke like scattering bats,
Shop life's dreams away,
In the punctual errands
Of life's grid of mundane horrors,
Relish the end of the day,
With a dry Chardonnay,
To relish your triumph,
On the NASDAQ swing,
And over the secretary.

I know about daycare and soccer trips,
And the corporate needs,
Of our family,
I hear the same alarm that daily brings,

Our lives to the command,
Of necessity and comfort,
As we pad silk pillows,
In our cage.

I yearn for truth, and small moments,
A heartfelt chuckle in the woods,
A touch of warmth,
When the chill sets in,
And a need to feel you,
When it is welcome.

Sail the man you love,
Pack him in your purse,
Run him on beaches like a mule,
Drink him under the table,
Rapture is not a recipe,
For the organized cook.

I remember a smile,
Like flattering leaves,
Falling in my direction,
That said mostly,
Be my friend.
You hurl down your heads on silver plates,
And dance your tease,
Pretending to keep up.
Do not ask me to be your mate,
It is not a good place to be,
When you are both.

I still want you in a taffeta dress,
Cooing like a bird,
Upon my mistakes,
But without a Harter in your manicured hands,
Of pink painted nails,
A fragrant rose curled in my sweaty hairs,
Of virtue and patience,
Behind that hanging mascara look,
That impales me,
With its thorns of white molten gold.

I long mostly for your touch,
On a bareback day of freshly cut grass,
With the dirt on your palms,
The laughter in your ruddy cheeks,
The falter in your poise,
As you pick the flower of your choice.

New Year's Day

On New Years' Day,
A young woman was folded in my arms,
A happy waif cuddled in a green sea of quilt,
Which led me to wander a bit,
About the rain, and the dew of a green meadow,
Swathed in the rays of a breaking sun,
Which like her blonde hair,
Caressed all life into being,
But for a moment stayed to watch,
The blossom of a young seed,
Ungrounded and immature.

The seed grew,
Like a patch of cherry bougainvillea,
Which sent away the sophisticate,
Who harps on the mechanics of relationships,
And the all-knowing expert was summarily fired,
From his position as society's bellwether,
Of dating,
No Cupid is he,
Who relies on the data of geography
To smite love,
In the interest of space and time.

As they talked,
The colors grew in colors of fuchsia and pink,
Like the cherry red of her lips,
And the glow of her perfect face,
Though tempered with memory's last longing,
Of a golden smile and olive eyes,
And a look of innocence,
That for a moment turned away,
My mind was made up then,
Its thoughts quickly relegated to that,
Dusty bin of rejection.

"You haven't called me for a date,"
Came as a resurrected missive,
Of heart worn Fate,
Which has tried my patience,
For a life of winters,
That rendered me numb to all sensation.
For once I am not jaded,
By the toil of would-be romance,
To not recognize the beauty,
Of a smile and the wonder,
Of pure laughter.

I heard the wood stumble in the fireplace,
Crashing dramatically near my glass of red,
Throwing sparks about a Persian rug,
And the flames that lit the kindling,
Burned a hole in my soul,
While you were away,
I miss you now for an instant of hurt,
That only distance will punctuate,
As the rain patters on my bedroom window,
And echoes on an empty bed.

What is it about you?
Your love of people,
Your independent thought,
Revolt against those stupid rules,
And fire me like a bed of hot coals,
What am I gonna do with you?
Who greets the homeless,
And every other living creature,
Because they are your friends.

Talk to me about the death penalty and dim sum,
And you cover the Great Divide,
Of all that is,
Render me speechless,
With talk of Camus and a ferris wheel,
That circles in holiday lights,
Like your child's eyes.

Kiss me here, and kiss me there,
But by all means kiss me,
For in you is a sea of pleasure,
That intoxicates every need and every want,
I touch you, and I am wondering already,
About climbing mountains.

There is static and distraction,
Beyond our love,
That keeps us in check,
Over a line of militant pawns,
That dares to complicate desire,
In our horizon the only black cloud,
Is the lightning storm,
That invites us to dance,
In the rain swept streets.

Jazz me up baby!
Pour me a drink,
Wake up to reality,
You are all the woman I want,
For in your straight arrow simplicity,
You are the girl,
Who on a bareback day of freshly cut grass,
With the dirt in her palms,
And the laughter in her ruddy cheeks,
And the falter in her poise,
Picks the flower of her choice.

LIMBO

A chord pulled tight between two screws,
That shifts the balance to and fro.
The wind that sweeps the ground below,
Upon which we dare to stretch our forms.
Bent knees, chin up, our bared bellies,
Suspended forward ready now,
To clear the passage wide and low.

A pendulum that swings from side to side,
Should lessen now its constant speed,
To a slowing cadence softening,
Bright and harsh reality,
To comfort's warmth and wondering.
Though yet Time accelerates all things,
In finite misbegotten deadlines,
Drawn across the page of life.

Watching, waiting, thinking,
The spring of yeses, nos, and maybe,
The soul's patience now wears thin,
Of hearing the conflict born within,
Hanging by one's nails is noble,
Until your fingered hands,
Become stretched like rubber,
Your feet hanging in that black abyss.

Decision is the bravest word,
From which there is no turning back,
Forge forward and with strong attack,
Placate the heart or common sense,
Or ruminate until your gums,
Bleed in streams of ambivalence,
The hourglass has no mercy,
Its sand pours down without delay,
No time for retrospection.

The man who searches for perfection,
Is likely to find an elegant room,
To which he can toast his solitude,
Near a warm fire of spitting embers,
Where he can dream of mild seduction,
But when the Bells of Time ring clear,
What will the eulogy trumpet here,
But the legacy of some decision?

LET HER GO

Let her go
No you don't get it
Let her go
But I love her
I love her
Let her go
She is my life
No let her go
No just let the belly go
There must be a way
It will come back
They always do
And so
The green eyes
The blonde hair
Let them go?
Why she looks great in a pair of stiletto heels
And tangos like the finest
Let her go
Because
She is fat
And you don't like it
She is not fat
She is thick
With wonder and love
For me
That I respond in kind
Like the air in an Argentine forest
To her trickles of goodness
Let her go
She must marry a man
That does not have this issue
And will love her wholly for what she is
Without surgery
Without diet

Without exercise
Let her go
She is my life, I rebel
For there is no one,
I promise you, like her
I cannot live here
I cannot breathe;
Without her,
Let her go
We will work on it
We will,
Hah, but for five years now
You could have built
The pyramids at Egypt in less time
Than it took to marry and accept
The physical cross you bear,
To bear now what is svelt and stupid?
Do you know what it is like to find
Her skinny counterpart with burdens more
Than a few pounds at the fore?
Damn it then, what happened here?
The photo sits upon my table clear
The smile, that smile so dear,
The miles of time we've crossed and borne
The support, the will, the comedy
Upon which our liaison was torn
The pewter heart upon my windowsill
Is enough to soothe my will
I love when she gnashes her teethe at me
I love the look of her eyes in the morning
Green irised wondrous bulbs
Like the eyes of children peering
For the first time on a clearing
Where a fine doe stands and watches
In a dewey meadow, there she is
Accepting me, and our history
Bad shitty little history
Unchanging insidious path
Engraved by heredity's wrath
God can't we go to some other place
Where Hollywood won't plead its case?

Cannot soul mates live in peace
And simply love, and love simply?
Let her go
No let me go.

HEARTS AND ARROWS

The jeweler downtown showed me the piece,
One point three carats
GIA certified with few imperfections
I think it was a D
When you looked down at it in the microscope
The angles were perfect
Six arrows, six quadrants
The beauty of it was stellar,
Like the galaxy connected by the dots of stars,
When it shown in the sun
It was bright, and colored
A Hearts and Arrows Cut
That reflected rainbows on those walls.

Cash, he said and I was off
Rushing to the bank on Broadway
I collected and guarded it
On that long walk back to the jewelers
I laughed distractedly about a return policy
I guess they don't refund love's folly
It was a beautiful ring, which she proudly wore
Until the arrows started to sling
That her beautiful face was just not enough
To make the passage.
A pewter heart remains
Tucked in my treasure trove of meaningful things,
Fossilized well meaning tributes
To what was but did not become.

No poetry of spirit, no force of imagination
Could resurrect what I had killed
A broken heart, but arrows
Still resolute and sharp.
It all died that one day
When she said goodbye

To the flowers and me
And whispered that she would never live here again
In the smell of the jasmine
Where the Lilies of the Nile bloomed stupidly

Like purple swabs of cotton
Over the sprinkled grassy green,
Like her eyes, and the glory of her smile
We kept on beating this dying horse,
Which for one year and more just languished
Focused on the thing that wrecked us,
Instead of the things that brought us near.

PARTY BOX

Hey, you, in a pinch.
I am positive today,
The dark blue skies of Malibu,
In the rainy season,
Marked my birthday.
Clouds suspended and pregnant
With madness,
A vast stretch of ice plant,
Red carpet to my dreams,
A rustic house whose first story
Was furnished with friendship,
The steaks are on, the fondue's hot,
The wine is good,

The conversation lively.
Toasts are made, a dog dances,
And spins in ecstasy
Smoke a cigarette with me,
Tell me how you feel,
And what you want,
And what you dream about.
Share your darkest secrets,
I will store them for you,
As I pluck the petals of a rose,
To find more petals,
Of so much fragrant complexity,
Give me a window view of the pouring rain,
From a warm and pointed bed,
While you whisper your thoughts,
Like wisps of ocean wind,
The sounds from beneath call
For more camaraderie,
I leave you to your slumber,
And go and play in the party box,
Zoning, whirling in expression,
Playing poker, and Morphine,
Hugging, loving and catching up,
While we banter chat about,
Too afraid to jinx
The beauty of all of us.

THE GARDEN

April rains upon this plot of earth,
Food for the innocent seed,
Triumphant in ambitious birth,
Near roots of crusty giant trees that lead,
The paths of hopeful sprouting dreams.

Green with ravenous appetite,
Elbowing through the ivy's crawl,
Unbridled hungry thoughts alight,
Basking in a new sun's rays that fall,
Upon the open realm of promises.

A gardener's shears soon discipline,
Libertine shoots of June's reckless weed,
That lust and grope and playfully sin,
Resistant with no rules to heed,
But the flat horizon of desire.

A hungry flytrap's sibilant tongue,
Eyes convention's tasteless snacks,
Energized by July's hot suns,
Escaping now the machete's hacks,
Its mission masked with uncertain smiles.

Bougainvillea learn to teethe,
Upon pretty frames of planted spikes,
But what is the trembling underneath,
These meticulous gravelled hikes,
If not the quiet rage of orphaned passions?

Wild ambitions neatly clipped,
Molded fancifully in animal shapes,
Leafy stoic gargoyles for a crypt,
Of hedge that walls the pained landscapes,
Raked clean of hybrid mischief.

Under the August shade of corroded eaves,
Trimmed consciences fester in wet heat,
The large oak spanning veiny leaves,
Under which darkened patches soon retreat,
To spineless, stunted mediocrity.

Creamy ponds suspend in animation,
Sticky dreams, and dragonflies,
Complacent in their current station,
And satisfied by the compromise,
Of ideals ebbing in the mud.

September stepping stones now in place,
Cement quaint trails that invite,
Caution, care and the proper pace,
Or panicked, scuttling leaves in flight,
Whispering quiet wisdoms.

The chilling fog of the December morn,
Enshrouds proud trunks in its cotton quilt,
Whose naked limbs reach out forlorn,
With hardened claws and knots of guilt,
Screaming out in strained surrender.

Silent could-have-beens still breed,
Wandering, aimless regrets that stumble,
Like the garden's topsy-turvy tumbleweed,
But in its weathered carcass still does grumble,
The echo of an angry wind.

There must be time to cultivate,
The sweet remnants of autumn's rot,
Chance will come to irrigate,
This quaint and sordid burial plot,
Covered in the withered leaves of hope.

For I dare not uproot, I shall not disturb,
This dignified bed of bloody marigold,
And searching, strangling herb,
That carpets this rocky ground so cold,
To retrieve my soul.

ARLETTE

A young blonde lady with shapely legs,
That in their spindly heels left their staccato imprint,
On the sidewalks of Houston and Paris,
And declared, "Bonjour, ca va?"
The loud inquiry rising up like a wake-up call,
With an expectant smile of someone,
Beleaguered but fighting,
Coiffed and ready and beautiful,
Standing straight and sassy,
Who knew life, the bearing of children,
Two continents and a world of anguish,
A rich, blue scarf fluttering above a perfumed scent,
That announced the advance of royalty,
The raucous laugh that cut through the pose,
And delighted in the human farce,
Though often brooded in inertia's indecision,
To whom I read the Cards and said,
This is it,
Don't pin your hopes on a different kite.

A family tree dictated that,
Arlette would always be there.
She was young until one day,
She died.
The slashing repartee and commanding voice of the Troubles,
Hello, I am not feeling well,
Yet again.
How many pills are you up to,
Now?
Think it away,
Just like you invited it.
Your germs, your indigestion,
Your fainting spells on the bathroom floor,
One more time,
Cry wolf!

And when the bitterness and routine indifference,
Sounded no bells,
Though you spat up blood and became,
Pale and weak,
And grabbed your dying abdomen,
In some Paris clinic,
Where doctors idly watched.

Your stomach ache,
Turn into gangrene,
Before their very eyes,
And relegated your life away,
To some mystery bacteria,
That reveals itself when,
All other answers fail the question,
Of *why?*
No eyes of knowing support to see you through,
No warning that you were about to,
Slip away,
In your room of silence,
So terribly alone,
Unknowing and hapless,
An anesthetized goodbye.

O death you are worse,
When you arrive without so much,
As a calling card.
We poor humans reel then unprepared,
For mourning,
Accusing and pecking away,
Like vultures.

How nice was that bistro,
In the banking district,
Weeks, no, eons before,
The chatter of family talk,
The common sense decisions,
Of what to do and who to marry,
Who spoke critically of family members,
As she would of me,
As close friends are inclined to do,

A perceptive merciless eye,
That always showed you mercy,
And gave you reams of advice,
That she could not herself follow,
Because she enjoyed your company,
"Et le prix des bananes?"
"Et les fromages?"
What joyous celebrations of being,
Someone clear,
And indefinable,
And full of spunk.

A goodbye umbrella in a rainy alley,
Of Ile de La Cité,
Lonely and loved,
It was blue, like she was,
But not nearly as electric,
You did not simply exist,
You were life's energy,
I am at your side,
Forever.

WHEN I DIE

When I die I hope that I survived,
Myself,
All the drinking and smoking days that became,
An excuse to live completely,
When I die I hope that I will have tried out every dream,
Writer, lawyer, photographer and painter,
Real estate developer, carpenter, and teller of long tales,
Father, brother, son and man,
And maybe husband if that thought awakes me,
When I die I hope,
That my progeny will come from every source,
Writing, children, thoughts,

That affect the world after me,
When I drink I see that I can do it all,
But sober me finds faults at every junction,
When I die I hope,
The world is less embattled than today,
Though bloodshed and famine will rule the way,
Of any dreamer that has not placed,
A selfless eye on the human race,
When I die I hope that articles are published,
That ideas and rallies go recognized,
At least to feed a generation's battle creed,
That you existed and were somehow noticed.

As an Older Man I Walked

As an older man I walked,
Down the dirt roads of a field,
Of wheat and black crows,
That led to the unknown abyss,
Of unshakable loneliness,
The only thing left alive,
Was my pumping heart,
Which does not know when to stop.
Its clockwork dribble of old blood,
It was my reply to life's enigma,
Defensive, and defenseless,
To time's march,
Of budding seeds to leaves browned,
By this winter cold,
Were it that we were evergreen,
Resting for the next bout of spring.

I nap upon my California King,
In a vacant home,
On a night after that drivel of work
That is my life's calling,
Or that I called my life,
A strange conundrum that makes,
The clicking sounds louder,
The only creaks that frighten me
Are not the ghosts of haunted homes,
Or vicious murderers walking lightly in the shadows,
But the clutch of despair,
As we die.

No happy timetable,
Of Medicine's great reach,
Can prolong the lives,
Of our loved ones,
Ten and a few years perhaps,
But they are seventy,
Down a dark stretch of road,
I start waiting for the call.

I hear my father's thoughts,
Of friends come and gone,
Like the brown leaves of autumn,
Flying from their limbs,

Gone away on Saturday,
The scratched out names of an address book,
Numbers like doodles on a pad,
Disconnected.

I cried at the age of six about the call,
That my parents were not eternal,
Thinking then in my muffled guilt,
Of my mother in the kitchen,
Crying too, who had lost her own,
I did not say a thing,
I wrote to you later,
I received your reply.
I do not pretend to know what it is like,
To have memory reduced,

To a wooden casket or a porcelain urn,
For it is impossible,
To find them there.
I do not conceive of small talk at wakes,
That could massage indefinable pain,
A gravestone is a piece of rock,
That never lived.

This weekend, John Spence, eloquent orator,
Of cases of welfare fraud collapsed,
On the track of a Five-K walk,
Maybe 58, I can still see his elocution,
Righteously about practically nothing,
But well-versed in public speaking,
Older than Jeff, who was my age,
Who found his last moment,
On a basketball court,
With two kids and a heart attack,
Or Marty, who told me to buy,
The most expensive house I could afford,
Who after being handed divorce papers,
In ICU twenty years ago, after his bypass,
Bellied up over take-out pizza,
At least they didn't go like Gail,
Who within one month of her retirement
And a new house in the mountains,
Choked to death,
On a piece of meat.

You stalk us in the forests of Kansas,
You hover in the cancer wards,
You pop up at a freeway in rush hour,
You make your house in our bodies,
And then develop acres.
On occasion you announce yourself,
Like a gray cloud that whispers,
"Here I am, my soon departed,"
And plays coyly with emotion,
You are faxed in cryptic notices,
Attention demanded in the workplace,
Of a boss who passed,
That once shook your hand,

For sending another to the same fate,
Who now dallies on the same row,
As the rest of us,
Waiting, and watching
Time's cheating trickle,
Probate's assistant,
Taunting you,
To wind things up,
Salivating like a breathless hyena,
For that stroke of lightning,
Floating on that black horizon,
Readied like a razor.
We gauge our chances against you,
The cigarettes, the booze,
Red meat, and every care in a world of chaos,
Though the headlines' favorite boast,
Is the fire down the street,
The airplane's fatal fall,
The innocent of the West Bank,
The scourge of Africa,
And Toby at five had yet to smoke,
When that truck came along.

We become misers with our minutes,
We forgo life to put you off,
Forget the mountain hike,
The river ride, the sail around the world,
Ignore the need to reach the precipice,
For fear of your intrusion,
Scuttle the bravery and good will,
To the attic of well-meaning episodes,
We mine our moments,
As if to conserve a species.
We invest our days,
Like shares in a stock portfolio,
Glancing over our shoulder,
At the stream of vertical sand,
Pouring through your hourglass,
So that we may live longer,
But less.

We can gauge our chances,
And buy a few beers at your poker table,
We can duck your spades,
For hearts and diamonds,
But we can never check,
A game that is played,
To the House's end.

Who are you?
Just the name we give to,
States of being,
Like life, which is a word,
That defines beauty and love,
And a pulse,
While you are a blackened gargoyle,
A dark horse-drawn chariot,
But merely the face we apply,
To the grief that one spent heart brings,
When the beat is gone,
We must call you the Angel of Darkness,
For human loss is a horror,
That defies all.

Dear death, my dark friend,
With all your drama,
You are helpless,
For your shadow,
Would not exist but for a sun's bright light,
You can squelch the beat of the drum,
But never the music that it spawned,
You can remove the source,
But not its progeny,
You can suffocate the voice,
But never deafen the ears,
You can kill the teacher,
But the students will rise against you,
Blood may dry,
But memory forges a line,
That you can never cross.

Black and Tan

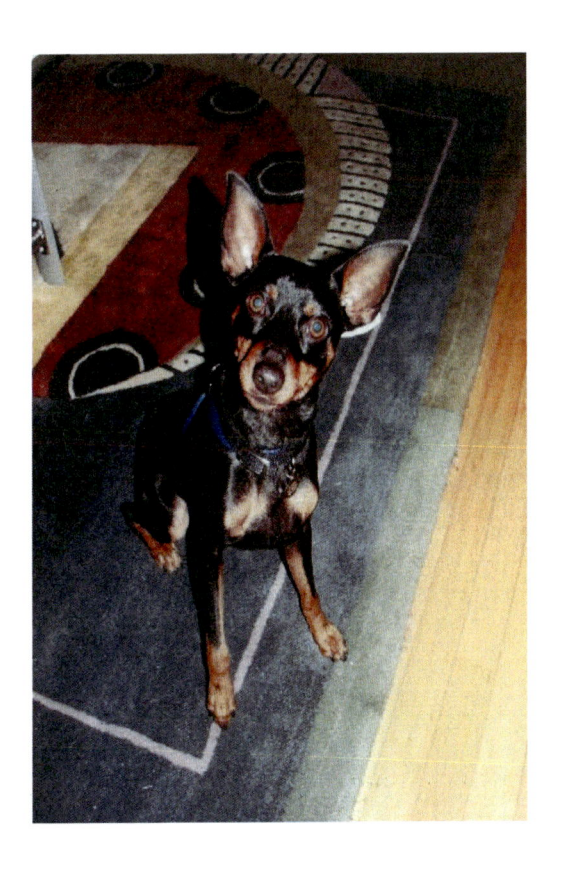

Miniature is but a euphemism
For your bark is bigger than that spaniel's retort
My whippersnapper jingoist
You had the six-foot utility man in his sneakers trembling
Highly annoyed by this occupational hazard
Of little dogs behind backyard gates
That announce with a sign then ferocious presence
Enameled toes of ebony delightfully
Manicured by pavement walks
Hunting scented spirits with pointed nose
Trotting and deftly tracking head to the earth
What affection is better than your curled up body at my feet
Or the cool touch of your seal skin fur

Shrouding my shoulder, feet beneath
Or relentless kisses in the morn
Which demand a trip around the bend
To do your business in the mist
Of some landscaped yard of freshly cut grass
Scouting trunks and flowers
You've left unmarked in all your trips.

I feel bad when the New York Times does not arrive
Not for its distressing headlines
But for its blue wrapper now reserved
As a bag for surprises that you're soon to leave
On the immaculate lawn of the household from Japan
A bit of rustic brown feng shui to add a bit
Of color to this unhappening street.
You come to me at this keyboard, paws and licks, standing up
With that cropped tail wiggling in ecstasy
Your little butt tanned like a Coppertone model
Connected to spindly muscled legs
That in full run resemble
More the canter and confident gallop of a thoroughbred
Prancing head held high
The wombat ears turned back and tuned
To every silent whisper of the wind
With your cobalt harness always on
To allow me to grab you from the door
Before you eat the good Girl Scout
Before you chase down some female in heat
Husky, lab or mix, no retreat
Or cat, or motorcycle, postman too
Gender type will not defeat
Fixed, they look at you with bygone eyes
Like an old dowager reminiscing,
"He would have been good for me once,"
Like the little Chihuahuas on the safe side of Joe's wall
Yapping, running, jumping
Like a trio of energetic appetizers.
We call them, "Breakfast."

I remember that scalding day at the gas station
That registered 110 degrees on a Palm Springs afternoon

You and I were looking for second homes
I left you in the gassed up car
Running idly with a full tank, at the exit
To merely check the gas cap's position

I headed back to the driver's door
And stood frozen like an ape in shock
Discovering now that the car was locked.
By your friendly disposition
With you inside in deathly panic
Caged by actions a trifle independent

No access in, the windows shut, the engine running
I yelled for some attendant
But my Triple A card sat secured
With my wallet and cell phone
On the seat in the locked machine
That was my car and soon to be
The latest Max latrine
I wondered, "This can't be so bad,"
Until I felt the scorch of the Palm Springs sun
And then thought of my dog well done
Upon the scalded leather
So I remembered the day when my escape artist had
Brought down the windows and leapt mad
One paw touch and the windows down
Off you were, and the pavement's sausage
Not hurt at twenty five miles per hour,
But did you learn as much with that departure
As you did to lock your coffin?
Ideas soon swirled in crazed imagination
Where inconvenience ripens soon to panic
I began to jump from side to side
Around the hood to catch your attention
You, my Max, leapt inside the car
Obeying my theatrical direction
Left to right and back again
You tried to jump through the rear window
But the glass held you back
The dashboard was your counterattack
But then your paw by accident found

The rear side window that went down
A small triangle through which I squeezed
My full body with feet and knees
Only to find while grappling
That the keys were out of reach
Now to see that one mistake
Was made the worse by the handbrake
Which you triggered with much affection
In a downwardly direction
Thus me and Max, at the helm
Glided into traffic's realm.
If not for Palm Springs' finest
Where would the Beemer have come to rest?
The only question that I now picket
Who the hell gets the ticket?

My Olympian black and tan
I found you howling at the moon
Crying, I think, "Where is my friend?"
Outside of that patio door when in the evening
The creeping shadows and gusts of wind
Make us feel so terribly lonely
One wonders what the real Dobies are like
Is their activity more diluted
If spread out upon that bigger frame?
Are they frenetic too, desperate and jumpy?
Do they leap three times their game?
I imagine they might hit the ceiling
You almost do
Airborne through a door finally opened
A burst of motion like a jack-in-the-box
Energy left bottled for a work day, made combustible
By my arrival, and the open house's warm greeting
Triggered simply by the rattle of my house keys.

What do you think about, Max?
Where is your mind when you sit curled up
After leaving your silver bowl
With some beef jerky hanging from your mouth
As you meditate upon your blue comforter
Thrown down one day in the office

And left as a permanent piece of dog furniture?
Until you, my unconditional friend
My Sir Licks A lot
Comes to my keyboard with his paws clinging
Disrupting my process of deep pointless thought
To look upon me with brown searching eyes
And climb upon my chair and grab my neck
With those spindly outstretched arms
Clasped around my neck, clinging for dear life
As I do.
Perhaps with more decorum.

Connection Lost

I watched my lunch today,
Drenched in that crisp sunlight,
Of a Monday afternoon,
Streaming onto my desk,
Through my office window.
Bell peppers, yellow, green and red,
Basking in basmati rice,
The grains floating in my olive oil,
Like microorganisms.
A rainbow lunch, tasty and crunchy,
One mouthful and that's it.
That is all that for now exists,
The beheading of a wartime hostage,
The tango of two dancing lovers,
The spearing of a pepper by a fork,
One spinach leaf on one plate,
Between four walls,
In a building of reinforced concrete,
In a city of millions,
Drenched in that sunlight,
Of a Monday afternoon.
And then there is a sound,
Tap! Tap! On a tile floor,
As my foot patiently speaks,
To no one but me,
That now is all that exists.
A soft sound,
Of optimistic footsteps,
Walking, calling, trying to connect.
To the path of other footsteps,
That for now belong to someone,
But tomorrow will be their children,
Marching with trombones,
In perfect lines, like soldiers,
Beating drums and trumpeting,

With wide and fearful eyes,
Determined, playing, commanding,
The performance of your *to do* list,
For the day.

Echoes of a dream no less real,
Than this hard desk or that soft mango.
I feel them now, I smell them now,
But I do not understand them.
In the corridors of my mind,
Is an uncovered manhole,
Into which, for brief moments, I fall,
You might call it the Valley of Nothing,
Or the Abyss of Existentialism,
Or the Chasm of Madness brought on by,
Rootless Solitude,
It's just that in the recognition of things,
Is the awareness of their meaninglessness.
Like your spot in the parking garage,
The more you know the way,
The less it means.
Or the freeway with its lanes,
Like capillaries, heading here, and there,
But always heading home, this house.
To which I wander,
Sometimes completely by accident.

Metal keys unlock the front door,
Surrounded by two overgrown ferns,
That bray in the breeze,
Like a pair of donkeys,
And I close it behind, no lock this time,
In case there are guests or parcels,
Or a child politely asking for his ball,
That he kicked over my back wall,
Or perhaps a ghost that can give form,
And answer the rhetorical questions,
That swim in my head.
No scotch tonight,
Better to soberly note,
What it all really looks like, today.

No, just me tonight, here in,
Is it Los Angeles?
They gave this place a name,
Though it is no one,
But when the weather is bone chilling,
I can feel at least that.

As I see that I shiver,
And the wood is hot in the fireplace,
And I can feel that,
In my outstretched palms,
Or wrapped crossways around my chest,
I can almost feel a hug,
And Stravinsky is playing,
And I can hear that,
And the acoustics seem,
Fine enough for a recital,
But my listening to music,
Will not affect the world,
And will go unnoticed,
Except by the African masks,
That smile on my living room walls.

I always wondered if a tree makes a sound,
In the woods when it falls,
And you are the only one to hear it.
I prefer to sleep away the questions,
Than answer them with the screams,
That sometimes at night,
Visit my windowsill,
Mistaken by neighbors,
To be the whistling wind.

HOLES

Traipsing through happy morning clearing,
When the coffee is hot,
And the morning dew glistens with the dawn's yellow light.
And the car goes rum rum,
And the coffee cup is in its holder,
And Rachmaninov plays on,
Around the intersection where,
There are sometimes potholes,
In the street,
And in your being where the car falls, and your soul falls,
And plummets in the darkness,
And you have to climb up,
(Again)
To stave away the wall of tears that,
Like Niagara,
Come flowing through a broken dike,
Of, yes, your being.
Something not repaired,
And getting bigger,
As the dam tries in its concrete façade,
Not to break,
Entirely,
But in small forays of large bottles of wine at night,
That warmth and comfort and guilt.
Your inaction,
Of coming so far and just, just,
Stopping.
Why?
I don't know, and I care too much to wonder,
Why.

CONTROL

It's mine,
I worked for it,
So I could be free of it,
Like that cushioned green stool I conceived,
Please don't sit on it,
It just fills another space,
I installed Italian leather in my palace front,
Watch your drinks, like stray clawed cats,
That wander upon the suede,
Don't plant your heels on that Bombay chest,
You might scuff it,
Have a fun drink,
In the other room.
Chill the banter outside,
The neighbors might wander,
The hot tub is great,
But be wary of the levers,
They cost me months of impatience,
And plastic cups are great on the patio,
Because my Crate and Barrel cocktail glasses,
Are hard to replace,
As you are, who never breaks,
Spend some time, but not too long,
I must rollerblade,
Drift a bit but not forever,
I need my private space,
Caved in its four cornered walls,
So I can sing alone,
And clean my palace in its aseptic stare,
But bring your warmth occasionally,
It will help the hardwood,
A chess game?
If you put the pieces back my friend,
Who plays chess,
And darts and croquet,

But only when I say?
Just a four-person dinner party,
No chairs for more,
But come later for drinks,
When demons are gone,
When the only point to Italian leather,
Is the people that sit in it.

Oh, go forward with your home improvement,
Adorn this selective shell,
Its insistent poppies coloring the new rock wall,
Refi that and landscape this,
And glorify your production,
As your ego sells tickets,
To the next event,
About you.

From Makassar

From Makassar the road goes inland,
The van trundling down potholed roads,
Passing through drab country scenes,
A brown river here, a local market there,
Dried fish hanging like dirty rags,
One lies on my lunch plate in a vacant,
Restaurant, accompanied by soup and fried rice,
Always fried rice,
Western civilization's egg is laid,
In gas stations, tire stores and cement mills,
I start reading my epoch novel,
Of the Greeks and Spartans in the Pelopponese,
Terrifying tale of wartime strategy,
More provoking than the sites I see,
Whizzing by through the van's windows,
Nothing particularly interesting,
But the sounds of pigs squealing in Torajaland.

A gated tollbooth announces my visit,
Adorned with figures of bulls and boathouses,
I have arrived in Tana Toraja,
Gated by the summits of Kandora and Gandang,
Its valley blossoming gradually like a book,
Whose pages expand with illustrations,
Of greener hills and terraced rice fields,
And bulbous magical mountains that emerge.
From the flatlands that before,
Were less than postcard-worthy,
Now dotted here and there and upon the road,
Strange boat-like constructions,
That are the homes,
Of a civilization whose heritage roams,
Somewhere upon the sea.
Perfectly triangle rectangular in fashion,
Bamboo supports under the eaves,
The bow in front, the stern behind,
Wedges standing upon stilts, with great design,
Burnished by artistry of orange and brown,
Boasting water buffalo horns up and down,
The better the class, the higher the horns,
I hear the pigs squealing in Torajaland.

The mist hangs magically like a shroud,
The valley's dusk licking boathouse roofs,
Curled in rows against each other,
The long silent waters of a lagoon,
That stretch to the base of green mountain hills.
Terraced rice fields across the valley,
Where the dead sleep in caves that dot the cliffs,
And Tau Tau effigies stand as sentinels,
Vigilant puppets that stare down to connect,
The world with the hereafter,
Do you recognize Mother in her dress? Is that not Uncle Jeremy,
With his stern gaze that still accuses from the heavens?
They stand together on a balconied cliff,
As if watching with binoculars,
The opera of life,
Except when huddled in the darkness of the black cave,
Where above a row of blanched skulls and human bones they testify,
Silently.

White skulls, brown dirt, white rock.
Breadfruit tree trunks in carved prepared crypts,
Preserve the remains of infants buried,
Facing the direction of the families that mourn,
So up and away from predators,
That they become part of the tree.
I hear the pigs squealing in Torajaland.

The marketplace rustles with cocks to sell,
Flamboyant soldiers for a fight,
Beans and spices and fish so fresh,
That they jump into your bag,
Coffee, hot peppers, tomatoes, and bread,
Snakes writhing in barrels,
By the rows of peas and corn,
Glistening in the darkening sky.
The market opens to a clearing,
Where stands a herd of mighty buffalo,
Watching proudly the noisy fanfare,
Worth their weight in gold,
And auctioned off accordingly.
An echo murmurs above the din of buffalo sales,
The pigs are squealing in Torajaland.

In the humidity and mud,
I traipse past the squealing tied up pigs,
Down a corridor to Toraja houses framed around a killing field,
Their boatlike structures pointing inward,
As if to outdo each other,
The Alek Todolo of life reigns,
As repayment for gifts received,
A funeral procession of golden ladies parade by,
Dressed in saffron finery, red and yellow threaded,
Offering tea, in white porcelain cups,
Graciously we sit and enjoy the offerings,
Near the coffin of the great woman who died,
In a small decorative house that points its bow,
Towards the dusty arena.
Her husband handsomely dressed sits nearby to attest,
Upright, solemn, upon a platform.,
Laying on wooden slats and tied at wrist and ankles
Are the pigs,

Moving, brimming, quite alive,
To Torajaland the funeral cry.

Amidst the gong rhythms and folkloric dance,
Chanting, circling the buffalo,
Who is now down, and skinned and dead,
His coat now folded and hanging,
From the rack of a motorbike,
Departing, a trophy dragging on a dirt road,
His bleeding carcass now lays peeled,
His open eyes gazing in space,
So much ceremony for life's end,
A water buffalo to spend,
I hear the pigs squealing in Torajaland.

While the ceremony rages,
The wriggling pigs on bamboo poles are taken,
To a place behind the stadium,
The forest shadows cover the grand finale,
So the squealing pigs can have their say,
A warm and scarlet stiletto drawn,
From the left hind leg to release the soul.

While girls truss their coiffed hairdos,
Chatting of homage and cooking the beast,
With entrails now coiled like a sailor's rope.
The feast goes on for days on end,
Of pork and buffalo,
A new life's foyer in death's procession,
Much celebrated.

The van trundles back down potholed roads,
Where mountains flatten, and commerce thrives,
Dead fish are hanging in fast food marts,
And Syracuse has fallen.

But in Sulawesi life, the marble eyes,
Above the din and grind of market noises,
Are watching me from cliffs, rejoicing,
While in the misted dusk near Makassar,
I hear the pigs squealing in Torajaland.

The Walls of Rhodes

I drank somberly at an Old Town tavern.
Fortified I was against the New,
The glitzy bars so tourist bright,
That spat me out without a bite,
The Austrian couple on the square,
In leathered skin and cotton white,
A pair of aging mannequins,
With spritzers, manicures, and espadrilles,
Her makeup melting on the plaza,
Like the icing of a wedding cake,
Posing in elegance,
Exuding class and condescension,
While he instructed me on the fine art,
Of covering my bread,
From the ravenous pigeons.

I managed the journey from the Turkish coast,
Where drug dogs sniffed at the ferry's post,
The small port of Bodrum allowed the passage,
No varied routes were laid to exchange,
By animous cultures left so estranged.
My luggage was equipped with wheels,
Not made for cobblestone's appeal.
When the Isle of Rhodes approached,
I found myself in a new dimension.

On foot with baggage on my back,
I trekked through a maze of walls intact,
To a French inn preordained,
Thumpety-thump, and my back was sprained,
But a welcome beer brought me right back.
"Comment allez vous?" asked my host Jacques,
I said, "Not so bad," Amstel in hand
And took in a view from town to sand,
The anchored ships stood at attention,
At the pebbled paths' conclusion.

Showered now, I donned my shorts,
And hiked my Byzantine way,
To a touristy café,
That stood witness to a statued fountain,
Dry it sat around a set,
Of weary youth with readied backpacks,
And cameras clicking everywhere,
Of coiffed shoppers stumbling with shopping sacks,
And children braying for ice cream.

There we sat, or me and they,
Campari's enroute and watching the square.
Germans, British, Italian fare,
Chatting about their underwear,
The beautiful waitress at the alfresco,
Should've been from Italy,
Instead of street propaganda,
Of the richest sense,
She seated me with a Sophia smile,
To a lonely plate of pasta.
Linguine, I think,
That slithered like rich worms.

Surely there were treasures to find,
An Odyssean amphora?
No, it was a vase,
Made by some well-known artist.
Who I do not know.
With that helmet,
Of Trojan times,
That recalled that twenty-year war
When heroics bristled at the core.

A stone's throw here,
Would confuse these paths,
That whimsy their way under portals,
And shadowy corridors,
The marker for the turn,
Is the pink bougainvillea.
Then there is the laundry and the bar,
A restaurant's tables sit ajar,
Waiting for the night.

Licensed by Viguoli's pen,
An island found its gallant men,
In an outpost of a civilized sea,
Entrenched in the twelfth century,
Religion found its hapless whore,
In the bloodshed of a war,
Where the Knights of Rhodes found their stake,
A rock upon their vows to break.

I will not travel from these walls,
From this dark cocoon that is my right,
Proudly I will stalk the night,
"Thank you sir,"
Was so nice,
From a town that belongs,
To a world I do not tread.
Just my old walls to secure,
A lonely pain that does endure,
A grain of sand upon a beach,
Glistening without a reach,
The sun imbues my eyes with green,
A guise to a black and onyx sheen.
I forbid for I am forbidden,
To escape these walls so high,
Unless I choose from them to fly.

But what about the bartendress?
A tequila shot we shared in bliss.
Attractive, and mordant Cyprian,
Waiting for things to grow ripe,
Almost, but not quite, the James Bond type.
And there was Johnny spouting his art,
In muffled speech that spoke of beer,
An expat true but with no skill,
Who the drink at twenty-five would soon kill,
Destroyed so soon, for what walls I wondered,
That bottled his youth.

To this island once possessed,
By Europe's brightest youngest best,
Who, with their chaplains helped the poor,

With absolutions at the fore,
There the Church ordained its proclamation,
It was a port of great intention.

What do now the floodgates open?
But shopping hordes of tailored men,
And their brides sniffing comfort,
Their stares droop down like icicles,
Over the cobblestoned resort.

Where now solitary shall I go?
But to the tourist streets below,
Is there no freedom from the night?
Upon a gelding shall I alight?
Is there no freedom of expression?
The ramparts solicit invitation,
What is the one that ends it all,
To what chasm shall I fall?
I would like the crowds out there,
Not to recoil from my air,
Like horses in their grimaced fright,
Driven mad by evil light.

The Colossus where it once prayed,
Apollo's shadow has not stayed,
To cast its doubt upon the age,
Where goodness fought upon the stage,
Or was it Power's indecision?
That left the Templars to their fate?
Independence has its price,
All islands will be sacrificed.

I hear the echoes of distant times,
Made by the whispers of silent rhymes,
Pebbling past the sunlit portals,
There dined and drank the stalwart mortals,
Of Inns of Tongues from lands afar,
Where hearts of men once stood ajar,
Is it now the right position,
To now claim with deep reflection,
That In Christian brotherly embrace,
Rooted darkness made its case?

What prey tell does Lindos beckon,
Is it Athena's temple soon I reckon?
But I hear the Turkish siege impending,
That turns the key of souls now ending,
Down and farther down the stony canyons,
That imprison good intentions.

Forging forth to open gate,
Like a flood of human fate,
Only to recoil from the moat,
That encircles hope remote.

Through an archway in the dark,
Where life itself shined so stark,
In night's starry calculation,
I am witnessed by the night.
Up a street where mopeds roam,
I find a sign that sends me home,
To an inn up winding stair,
Where up top lies my Sultan's lair,
Batten down the windows, lad,
From the winds that whistle mad,
Across the tiled roofs just below,
A cat scurries to and fro.

In my deepest depths I think,
That we always fight upon the brink,
Goodness is a salamander,
Its colors change and soon meander,
The fight for good knows no end,
When the dirty rest the sword must tend,
No triumph lies in good intentions,
When the motive is soon replaced,
By power's merciless ascension.

My ocean rumbles like a battle creed,
In the echoed gallop of a steed,
Its harnessed teeth gnashing so white,
Crusading, fiercely at lightning speed,
Sweating shining hair and mane.
A whistling wind in the night,

Where is the path of good intentions?
Rock and sweat and blood soaked stone,
The ghosts of hooves that still now roam,
Saddled by some armored knight,
Gleaming hero of white light.

THE DEAL

The life is strong,
Whippoorwills of indecision bat around my brain,
Of a 40 year old-hum-drum-what-else-is-next existence,
Life reminds you of so much more than you do,
It kicks you in the stomach in the morning,
To guilt you into wondering *what else,*
This second, this minute you could be doing?
It stands in memoriam at every highway ramp and every poor fucker,
Whose only way was straight out of lockup,
Of a life that was used, and is missed.
Now, this particular moment, unshared, this chance,
Gone on bits of minor disaster,
Small, "*Oh yeahs!*" that promise great push to the next turn.

Two or twenty, my dear almost always African American friend,
Take the deal, and save the risk,
Or go to Vegas and gamble,
You may win a little or you may go down,
I am sorry that I am finally the Man,
To tell you what your life is worth,
It's all in the manuals about you people,
A handy guidebook to numbers calculated in years,
Condensed to your market value,
One or two priors, another small qualification,
A probation officer bends my ear,
And you are done.

Why couldn't you have seen the light like I did?
That cold incandescent beam,
Like the North Star that beckoned the chosen ones,
To lead, serve and punish,
Like righteous Poseidons,
Weathering the black seas.

I find myself in a small vortex,
At the top of Power's pyramid,
Crouched and eyeing you wretches,
Vile, meaningless failures,
That feed this building its daily diet,
And give me sustenance,
Like carrion, so that I may fly,
And cast my blood red eyes,
Upon the weak and wounded,
What joy to relish the opportunities,
That lost hope provides.

THE VERDICT

It was a crisp voice that said it,
That Monday morning in 95,
When twenty-four comforted and determined eyes looked,
Across counsel table to Madame Clerk,
In a silence, where time stood still,
"We, the Jury," recited she,
In words that declared across the flowered carpet,
Under noses where reading glasses perched,
The Verdict.

Not a question of responsibility but fate,
That idled upon our words in argument.
Mere words,
The indignity of this,
The righteousness of that,
Soy Lao is dead, should we kill another?
I concentrated on a spot,
Where the pine on counsel table produced a knot,
Virgil's knife could have cut the silence,
Of that room, like the cuts upon his victims.

You console yourself with the probability,
That no jury of black men and women,
And one white airline attendant,
Could ever say anything but, "Life."
No parole, no freedom to change,
But "Life" firm and safe from conscience's pangs,
We all go about our lives again,
Without the pall of vengeance's gains,
They hung in silence for a weekend,
One grandpa played with his grandkids,
And deeply considered the Question.

Which word was it I could have said,
That might have put a rifle to his head?

Which phrase of persuasion could it be?
That opened both eyes for one long second,
Though blinded in one, we may still be,
Visionary and ruthless to the tee.
What is the bailiff smiling at?
Why does the judge look so concerned?
Why is it now after so much pain,
That my breath is stifled at the main?
"Death!" is the verdict read gloriously,
Not, "Guilty," or, "Life," or, "Twenty Years,"
But a word that sounds like a dull gasp,
No syllables to bite in elocution.
Just this Death thing that hung in the air,
With an odor that stuck to our ribs,
Our breaths quickened in shallow spurts,
This was now the ordained fate,
Not much there to congratulate,
To the living souls whose tongues,
Now wag and salivate,
To the raw meat thrown to the electorate
Be tough on crime, so tough on crime.

You pull the lever to that trapdoor,
You'll find your soul accompanying,
The miserable beast to his dangling fate,
And the only thing you hear,
Is your halting speech,
And the sound of his shackles.

The black detective's wife I hear,
Wanted to be the first to pull the lever,
The dark African woman of Kenyan stock,
Who watched me so indecipherably,
Not a crease upon her brow,
No question here of, "What has God wrought?"
Just plain and serious,
Not thinking now, "What, another innocent black man caught?"
But then retorted to the eleven,
"That's a slam dunk," with the zest,
Of a Hanging Judge from the West.
The black man abused by his own dad,

Said I have arrived but he has not,
Let him pay, for he is not,
Me.

There is a small officious despair,
That clings to the oak walls of the courtroom,
As you exit its great doors,
After you have killed someone.

Out to our lives again,
Having dispatched our duty,
Carefully, conscientiously, ceremoniously,
But something remains,
As we crowd into the elevator,
Was it shame?
Good citizens all, with fierce exacted revenge.
Exhausted, sure, but incomplete,
"Death," said the Clerk.
"Death," said we.
"Death," said I.

Our deliberations challenged and peaked,
The intellect inside,
Will continue to canonize with pride,
The judgment reached,
But one day when the appeals are done,
Lester Virgil will find his fame,
On the second page of the Times,
Where will we be?

When he killed her, I said,
He must have been exhausted,
I mimicked him, poor tired man,
After he stabbed her thirty times,
I saw her losing her blood as she walked,
And collapsed at the register,
Her life trickling from holes down her apron,
With which her hands were tied,
For seven dollars.

ESSAYS

Lifers

The California Men's Colony in San Luis Obispo County rests in the golden hills of the Central Coast of California twelve miles from Morro Bay, somewhere between the National Guard Headquarters and the charming city of San Luis Obispo. Cuesta College is nearby, a fairly barren community college campus that straddles the base of the mountain peaks that dot their way along the Montana de Oro mountain range to the their eventual climax, a large boulder known as Morro Rock, which sits in the Pacific Ocean in front of the sleepy seaside town of Morro Bay. At 7:00 a.m., Morro Bay is covered in fog, but the peak of the rock in its Pacific waters stands mighty. I left it in the background with a cup of coffee in my car, watching for the turn.

California Men's Colony, left. The stretch of azaleas along the entrance way was comforting.

The installation, with its barbed wire institutionalization, warns you with big signs not to bring weapons, alcoholic beverages, or cellular phones. I parked at the BPT space, which stood for the Board of Prison Terms. I could see the watchtower overlooking the grounds separated by two fences, both electrified. I approached the office with my boxes of files, each numbered with an inmate's classification: C-4325, D-98623. Other numbers connect these people with my county, A-039675 or A-057234. These are the case numbers that they were prosecuted under, and because they are only "A" numbers, instead of BA, YA, or NA numbers. It means that these cases are very old, from the eighties if not the mid-seventies. Now was the time that those murderers come up for parole. There are large files for each inmate, replete with police reports, psychological reports, and BPT recommendations. Each tells a story.

I met Mary Ann Tarasoff, the public defender, at the security entrance where we checked in our badges and the guards checked our lunch. I packed one yogurt, a peach, a bottle of water, and a sandwich of prosciutto. Somehow I knew that was important. Mary Ann was about 50, rode a Harley, lived alone in the outskirts of Santa Barbara, and as I soon learned, was an avid advocate for the down-trodden. I'm not sure I would call people that have bludgeoned someone beyond recognition with a bumper jack in a fit of anger, after putting them in the trunk of their car and dumping them in a park in Los Angeles, *as down trodden*, but there it is.

I got checked in through security, and I must say the treatment was better than any airport I have flown out of. In prison they still respect a badge. A cursory look at my laptop and peach, and the guards were satisfied. There were two rooms upstairs through the locked security gate, eventually my box on its wheels and my other baggage for the day got through. I set up my laptop in the coffee room across from the parole hearing room and reviewed the case, and drank a cup of coffee. I put my lunch in the fridge.

I met Parole Commissioner Tom Salton, and chuckled to myself about his name. He was a stout ex-sheriff from Tulare County and sported happy smooth cheeks and a frightfully good disposition. His role was to captain the proceedings, question the Inmate about his role in the crime, and to make the final decision as to whether the inmate was to be released on parole by setting a parole date. If parole was denied, the inmate was ordered to return for one, two, or, in truly hopeless cases, five years later for a subsequent hearing.

The other member of the panel was Deputy Parole Commissioner Dennis Jones. He had been around for a long time. He was seasoned, cynical and friendly. He had a nice gray moustache that reminded me of a beaver building a dam. He spoke of the prisoners in their post-conviction performance. He was the king of the prison reports. The 115's were serious violations, like manufacturing pruno in prison, an alcohol made from discarded fruit. The 128's were simply administrative, like the failure to get out of bed in the morning. Over a period of twenty years it is likely someone may not wake up on time.

But Dennis rules. Because if you have fucked up, you will be doing another two years.

We sat ourselves down at a long table in the conference room. Mary Ann Tarasoff, the defense attorney, sat on one side of the table next to an empty chair. She had prepared notes from the inmates' files, targeting positive accomplishments, and favorable psychiatric recommendations that might tip the balance in favor of release. In essence, she was there to plead for mercy on their behalf. Through blinds on a wall of windows you could see the prison yard below. On another wall the emblem of the State of California with its ubiquitous bear emblazoned itself above the table. A tape recorder sat on the table next to a coffee maker. Other than the whir of an oversized fan and the buzzing of several flies knocking themselves against the windowpanes, one felt the serenity of a classroom about to begin a lesson.

The first inmate was Anthony Reid. Serving a term of twenty-six years to life. It was a conviction of the first degree. Anthony is a proud black man, now in his forties. When he killed Paul Davis he was in his twenties. He knifed him to death behind a camper, because Paul got in his face. The story according to witnesses was that Reid showed up angry near a liquor store. He met some of his drinking buddies, who tried to hug him, but he said, "Don't fuck with me, mother fucker!" He was seen walking to the liquor store, peering through the windows looking apparently for the victim. He chased him with his buck knife, dragged him to the back of a parked camper, and stabbed him several times. The body of the man was found the next morning by passersby. The autopsy revealed defensive wounds on the hands.

Anthony Reid admitted the offense, but testified that Davis was a panhandler that lorded over the liquor store like a hawk. When Reid got there to get his retarded brother some milk Davis demanded some money and showed him his gun. Reid responded angrily to the extortion. A mysterious accomplice appeared, not seen by any of the witnesses, and started hitting Reid. In the raged blur of his memory Reid saw a gun, and began hitting Davis, dragging him to the curb where he apparently finished him off with several stab wounds to the chest.

Salton went over the proceedings with the inmate, pointing out some of the circumstances of the offense, and asked him why at this point in time he should be set free. Reid cast his eyes down, and in a pleading voice softly repeated a well-practiced mantra, "I am sorry. I think about it all the time. I know I shouldn't a done it. If I could bring that man back… I feel so bad. I've changed. If it wasn't like. . . I think it shoulda been a manslaughter. But I accept it. I do accept it."

Salton replied stolidly, "Well, Mr. Reid, you've been in for some fifteen years. The record here shows this victim was unarmed. And he had defensive wounds. And you took him to a place of concealment. What about that? How is that manslaughter?"

Reid looked up from his position and said, "I don't know. I don't know how he got 'em. I just see a blur. Fightin' with this other guy… comin' at me… I am guilty, yes. I know I am."

Tom Salton peered at me over his glasses. "Counsel, do you have any questions?"

Perusing the original police report, I noticed how several transients had been called to testify that Reid had appeared angry when he walked up, and the butt of a knife was seen sticking up out of his back pocket. I began my assault.

"Mr. Reid, don't you remember Lily Halpern? She was an acquaintance of yours. She told the police you appeared to be stalking Mr. Davis when you loudly demanded if anyone knew where he was. And you walked up to see if he had gone into the liquor store. You were the pursuer, weren't you, Mr. Reid?" Mr. Reid looked over at me, his ears turning red. "Those people never said nothin'. Lily…that woman…didn't say nothin' at the trial."

"But there was a Lily. Right?"

Caught, Mr. Reid retorted, "I don't remember no Lily." "And what about that mysterious man who showed up with a gun and then disappeared. Any reason no one ever saw him. Mr. Reid?" I asked. Reid sat silently. Salton interjected, "Counsel, why don't you direct the questions through the panel?" The irritated voice rebounded against the room's bleak walls.

I reframed my next question, "Would the panel please ask Mr. Reid if it would be fair to say he had an axe to grind with Mr. Davis?" Salton looked over at the inmate. This gesture was enough to comply with the protocol.

Reid looked down at his handcuffs with the intensity of a collector examining an item of rare antiquity. "I told you he acted like he owned that corner. I was tired of getting hassled when I went to the store." In South Central L.A., thugs got their payola by intimidating store patrons much like school bullies skimming lunch money from students in exchange for the right to go to class unharmed.

I looked at him over my lenses. "Is that why you brought a knife to the Seven Eleven?"

Reid meekly whispered, "I don't know."

Commissioner Salton interjected, as if he had his mind made up. "Are you finished counseI continued, "Could we please ask Mr. Reid, through the panel, if he feels bad about what he did?"Tom, rolled his eyes at the ceiling, breathed a sigh of impatience, and looked up questioningly at Mr. Reid. Before Reid had a chance to answer, Ms. Tarasoff, testily interrupted, "Objection. Do we have to retry the Defendant, your honor? He's already said he was sorry." She shot me a darting glance that said *just let it go*.I replied, "The circumstances of the offenses are critical, Commissioner to any determination of whether a parole date should be set."

Tarasoff would not go quietly. She replied, "If that was all that was important, we could sit and do these hearings 'til kingdom come and never get anywhere. You might as well just deny parole to everyone because they killed someone twenty years ago. There's no point in smugly sitting here with smiles on your faces asking if this guy feels bad if all you're gonna do is deny parole after reading the police report. "Tom overruled Tarasoff but his eyes told me to make it quick. "Mr. Reid?"Mr. Reid, his voice breaking, said, "Of course, I feel bad." The fan continued to whir in the corner, causing some of the prison paper to flutter as it alternated its semi-circular route.

"And did you feel as bad after you knifed Mr. Davis several times, killing him?"

"I said it was a goddamn blur. But… I felt real bad." Mr. Reid gave a frustrated appeal. The voices of several prison guards could be heard in the yard."So bad you left him to rot in the street until he was found the next morning?" I aimed accusingly.

Tom looked at me. "Counsel?" I concluded with a satisfied, "I'm done."

Adjusting his moustache, Commissioner Jones began his review of the countless psychological reports in his file. He explained the procedure to Mr. Reid. Mr. Reid listened intently as Jones pored over the voluminous third party memoirs of the inmate since he checked into the facility fifteen years ago. There were three 128's, one of which involved Mr. Reid fighting with another inmate in the prison cafeteria in 2003. It had the ribald touch of a food fight that had gotten out of hand. For Dennis Jones, it was the sure sign that Mr. Reid was not ready for the real world. Then there was the discovery of a can of pruno in Mr. Reid's cell. Mr. Reid had since acquitted himself well in a twelve-step program. But the final straw was Mr. Reid's refusal to cooperate in a plan for psychological treatment. For this offense, the board psychologists had ruled that Mr. Reid continued to pose a moderate risk in the community.

As Mr. Reid's chin dropped down to the collar of his prison blues, Salton announced in soft and comforting tones that parole was being denied and that a new hearing would be set in two years. They walked Mr. Reid out of the room in his shackles, while everyone scribbled the findings onto the inside of their respective legal pads. In the silence, you could hear the marks of the pen to the paper as we dictated the next biographical segment of Mr. Reid's existence.

The flies continued collecting on the windowsill.

In his heartland drawl, Salton announced a break and asked the parties if we had any objection working through the lunch hour. Everyone agreed. I headed quickly to my laptop, typed in the results, and hungrily finished off a strawberry yogurt, the kind that contained fresh pieces of fruit. I reviewed the story of Donald Hart, C-473467.

On September 4, 1983, Donald Hart's marriage started falling apart. His wife, Judy, had asked to take in Beth, a friend of hers, because she had split up from her husband. By all counts Judy and Beth had been close friends since high school. But things had started to get strange in the summer of 1983. Donald and his wife became distant, and he found that Judy and Beth were spending an inordinate amount of time together. Donald began to drink heavily, suspecting that the two women were having an affair. One night, after drinking at a honky-tonk near Sacramento, the two women, apparently drunk, told him to get lost as they left him standing in a dust cloud churned up by the wheels of their departing Ford pickup. Jealousy festered, and Donald Hart doused its flames with alcohol for the next three months. Each interaction between the two women cranked his drunken anger up one more notch until he moved out to stay with his parents. One late night he armed himself with an old .22 rifle and drove to his former residence. Stinking of bourbon, he kicked down the door and marched to the master bedroom, where he found his wife sleeping alone on her side of the bed. Reversing the gun on his chest, he yelled at his wife to wake up so she could watch as he shot himself dead. As Donald Hart recalled at the trial, Judy woke up and half asleep, told him to, "Go ahead."

For Judy, that was a particularly unhealthy retort. Her chest took three of the bullets at close range. A fourth traveled up her shoulder, up though her jaw line and into her brain. His wife dead, Mr. Hart reloaded. On his way out he saw Beth leaping for the phone from the couch. They found her the next morning bleeding from 14 bullet wounds, still holding the receiver in her outstretched palm. It was dead too.

Mr. Hart walked in escorted by the prison guard. The prison guard had the face of a man used to the routine of rounding up and walking prisoners. His face was round and puffy and positioned comfortably on a double chin. His bored façade belied the sharp and alert eyes that darted on his prey like those of an oversized mouse spotting a piece of cheese. By contrast, Mr. Hart was thin, his face was ruddy, and his blue eyes peered pleadingly at the officials sitting at the conference table where he slowly took his seat. But for the institutional blue denim shirt, he had that haggard appearance of a fisherman that had seen a wealth of days at sea, the wrinkles of a sun baked face making him appear a decade older than he actually was.

Donald Hart was forty-eight, and he had murdered at the age of twenty-nine, and he now looked sixty.

Commissioner Salton summarized the events that had brought Hart to the California Men's Colony. He concluded by asking Hart if there was anything he wanted to add.

Hart who had been before the panel on three prior occasions in the last seven years, began to melt into a wave of silent sobs when Salton reached the point where he had fired the rifle into his wife's chest.

"How…how…c-c-coo… could… I… I… ha-ha-have… done… somethin' like that? I loved her… I loved her so much. So much. I tried so hard to make it right. But she didn't want me no more." Tarasoff counseled him in a conference of whispers. Hart regained his composure. "It was in the summer. We took Beth in cuz she was havin' problems with her man. And then it jus' all started to change. Judy… she… I dunno… got sorta' distant. They did stuff together and didn't want me around. And you know… I started to ask around…. you know… to see what was up… No one said anything… but you know… a man knows… when his wife doesn't want to be with him and… I knew in my bones that she wanted to be with this woman."

"When did you start thinking something was going on, Mr. Hart?" Salton inquired.

"We went all three of us out one night. And we were drinkin' . . . and I know. . you know . . . it was all booze. And they started laughing at me . . . I mean it was *at* me . . . they were putting me down. And I got pissed. . . I mean a man knows when some woman don't want him anymore . . . Just drinkin' and laughin' at me. *Both* of them . . .. And I said . . . 'Why?' and Judy said, 'Oh, Bill, don't you worry about it. We're jus' havin' some fun.' But I felt like. . . so small. I hurt. I hurt bad. We had it out in the parking lot. They left me. I still remember their faces smirkin' and flirtin' with each other . . . they took off in the pick-up before I got a chance to do anything . . .. jus' took off down the interstate." Stanton's mind seemed to have traveled to a forbidden place.

"What were you going to do to them?" Salton peered upwards from his glasses.

Hart stammered, "Gawd, I coulda ripped 'em apart. I was so mad. But I didn't. I just started drinkin' bourbon. Mornin' til night. Mornin' til' night. I drank and drank 'til I couldn't see straight. And I finally moved out. Let those two lovebirds nest in their shit so I didn't have to see it."

Commissioner Salton asked, "And then what did you do, Mr. Hart?" A lull of silence filled the room. The coffeemaker brewed the last drops of its second pot.

Hart slowly continued, wiping away a teardrop that had rolled to a stop, glistening on the edge of his jawbone; "I kept on tryin' to deal with it . . . but I was just watchin' my life go down the drain. Everything I had built." Hart wailed. "Jus' gawn!" Hart gestured his hand across his lap in a weak, exasperated wave.

"And so I went over that night . . . I went to town with a bottle of JB, and I was feeling, well, pretty pissed off. I took the rifle. 'Cuz I was gonna shoot myself. But I first went over to the bedroom window, and peered in and saw Judy lying on my side of the bed, and I looked to see if anyone was next to her, and the sheets looked like they were messed up and stuff. And about that time Beth opened the door and let me in. Hell, I kinda barged in. And then I went into Judy's room and well . . . that's when I lost it."

"Counsel?" Commissioner Salton looked in my direction. I was poring over a transcript of Mr. Hart's last hearing.

"Mr. Hart, did you ever see Judy and Beth kiss or act in a romantic way to each other?" I asked.

"Aw, hell, sir, you could jus' tell. A man knows…and I didn't have to see . . ." Hart replied.

"You just sorta felt like they were having an affair?" I was unclear.

"I suspected something . . . :"

"And no one ever told you they *were*, right?" I emphasized that his suspicions had never even been comfirmed.

"No," Hart replied.

"And by the way, Mr. Hart, you didn't throw that part in about the bedroom window at the trial did you?"

"No! And I tell you why," Hart replied defensively. "I didn' want to piss off the judge. "

"You are telling us that you could've had an argument for manslaughter ....That you saw your wife in bed with someone else and you never thought of mentioning that to the judge?" I asked incredulously. "So now you've got yourself two first degree murder convictions and you want us to believe you were some poor betrayed husband whose wife was sleeping around with another woman?" I couldn't help myself.

"I told you. I went in there to kill myself. . ." Hart looked tired.

"With twenty bullets? Was that to make sure you didn't miss the first 19 tries? How many times ya' suppose, Mr. Hart, you'd have have to shoot that rifle at your head to get it right?" I had adopted my folksy pose. "I tell you it was like an urge . . . when she said 'You go right ahead,' and an uncontrollable urge swept over me ." Stanton explained. "And so you turned the rifle on her, as she lay there looking up at you from the bed? And you shot her?" I was addressing the Commissioner with my eyes but my rhetoric was aimed at Hart five feet in front of him.

"Yes. Yes." Mr. Hart looked defeated

"Six times. That was a pump action rifle, wasn't it?

Yeah." Hart replied. "But you had an impulse you couldn't control?" I inquired.

"Right. "Hart stared at a coffee stain on the conference table.

"And after you fired the first round at her chest, while she was dying, you loaded that rifle again?" I asked.

"Yeah . . ." Hart's answer sounded more like a yelp. "And you did that four more times, right?" I asked. Tarasoff interjected, "Objection! This is absolutely unnecessary. Mr. Hart has already served his time for this crime. Can we please stick to his rehabilitation?"

I vehemently countered, "Not until he has accepted full responsibility, Commissioner."

"What does he have to do make the D.A. happy? Sign his apology in blood?" Tarasoff's teeth gnashed furiously.

"I am so sorry. I am sorry. The pain of all of it. I think about it every day. Every day!" Hart rambled on.

"Continue, Mr. Prosecutor, but please finish." Salton looked at me impatiently.

"And when you were done with her you marched into the living room and leveled that rifle again at Beth. And loaded, pumped, and fired that gun fourteen more times. Was each of those shots also impulsive?"

Hart didn't know what to say, so he looked down at the cuffs around his wrists and chose to say nothing.

Commissioner Salton concluded my examination by inviting Commissioner Jones to make his remarks.

Jones droned on through the minutiae of Mr. Hart's psychiatric reports. In particular he emphasized the alcohol program Mr. Hart had just enrolled in. I mused that Hart deserved kudos for finally getting it right. He had accomplished the first three steps of a 12-step program on his twentieth year of prison life. Some inmates get their doctorates in philosophy in half the time, I thought.

Mr. Hart listened obediently to the reports. He hardly winced when Commissioner Salton stated that the Board of Prison Terms had concluded that the inmate continued to pose a high level of threat to society.

Tom Salton, in denying parole and setting a hearing date for the longer term of two years, stated that there was one fact of particular relevance to his conclusion.

It was the fact that Hart's five-year old son had been at the house during the murders and had slept through the ordeal. His father had left him to find the carnage in the morning. I wondered if this little scar had raised its ugly head in the child's adult life. He must be in his mid-twenties by now.

Commissioner Salton looked at Mr. Hart in disbelief, and said, "It was just all about you, wasn't it Mr. Hart? "

Exhausted, we wrapped up the day and drove to our respective hotels for the evening. I stopped at a restaurant on the oceanfront in Morro Bay and ordered a glass of Cabernet.

I sipped it while examining the fog's approach over a pink and blue sunset that reflected reddish sequins across the water. The air was cool. The sound of children could be heard in the background. It was family night at The Seagull, a restaurant that Tom and Dennis had recommended. I finished my glass at the bar while my table was readied, and chatted with a contractor about the pros and cons of building a house in San Luis Obispo County. The restaurant sported the usual sea theme everywhere; a marlin hung in front of me with its sharp snout pointing to the left. Food servers bustled about.

I dined on a dull fish while reviewing the cases for the next day.

In the morning I checked in my lunch bag and laptop with a female prison clerk as she waited on visitors. Tarasoff showed up on her Harley, nodded a civilized hello in my direction. We were escorted back through several electronically controlled gates to the hearing room. Salton and Jones were relaxing with their morning cup talking about fishing in the Sacramento delta.

Our next inmate was Mr. Joe Brabant. He was bumped up on the calendar because the inmate before him, a young gay Filipino, had stipulated to a two-year denial, as he had not earned his marks yet in his psychological assessment. Smiling, with the appearance of a fragile adolescent, the Filipino had been brought in briefly for his first hearing to discuss his culpability for the killing that earned him a second degree murder sentence; on the day of the crime he had apparently suffered a negative reaction when he was manhandled by his sugar daddy in the kitchen of their home; he responded by attacking him with an array of utensils, one of which was a sharp barbecue fork. It was clear from the young man's excited demeanor that his current regimen of psychotropic medications did not exactly chart the road to recovery. He was still smiling like a child at a surprise birthday party when they led him away.

Brabant, on the other hand was the epitome of the hardened criminal, a gruff white male in his forties, bulging with a muscular physique even as the stony contours of his face gave away his years. The steel blue eyes conveyed no emotion. He had a short mustache and seemed to clench his teeth as he addressed us with a surly, "Good morning". He was the only one who was serving a life sentence for a crime, which did not involve taking a life. He was being punished under a seldom used habitual criminal statute for perpetrating a take-over robbery at a McDonald's. Miraculously, no one had been hurt.

After Commissioner Salton reviewed the offense in detail with the inmate, Mr. Brabant gave a short speech where he touted the fact that in his career of serial property crimes not a single life had been taken. I was ready to order him a plaque for outstanding achievement in the community when I realized that an innocent bystander in the case had tried to play hero and almost gotten himself shot.

I asked Brabant about the mortal danger in which he had placed the customers of the fast food restaurant, to which he aggressively retorted,

"That's the problem with you guys. You don't know anything. The D.A. just comes down here and says the same thing every time. That guy was suing McDonald's for what happened. And he made it all up."
"Did he place the expended shell in the back of your car?" I inquired.

"No, but I didn't shoot at him. He comes flying out of the car where his kid was sitting and slammed the front door into Jacobs {the co-suspect} and sent him bouncin' into the parking lot. Then I gave the gun to Jacobs who I think gave it to Smitty. Then I don't know what happened."

"But you heard a gunshot?" I inquired.

"Yeah, but it was like a warning. And this guy goes running into a pole and now is trying to collect a few bucks." Mr. Brabant replied. You'd run away from someone too if someone was pointing a gun at you, wouldn't you, Mr. Brabant?" I asked with false curiosity.

Mr. Brabant sat silently and glared. The word, "Maybe," slipped through the small black opening his mouth formed between his clenched jaws. But he added, "I woulda jus' stayed put, sir."

Mr. Brabant was an expert on the subject. This was his fourth McDonalds' robbery. And wasn't because he had a penchant for Big Macs. He had worked at one and knew the peak times, the location of the safes and the restaurant's employee policy of no resistance. This custom had apparently not been shared with certain customers who were of the mind to protect their children and save the day, even at great risk to them.

"This wasn't the first time you committed a takeover of a McDonald's?" I began. "Depends on what you mean?" Brabant sneered back

"Well, let's just say that you figured you would encounter no resistance at this fast food place." I countered. "And you hadn't had any problems taking money from them before? Pretty easy pickings, wouldn't you say?"

"Objection, argumentative! Can we do without the drama?" Tarasoff railed.

"Counsel, wrap it up." Salton stated in a commanding tone.

I darted a glance at Salton. "A couple of questions more, please." That usually meant no less than a dozen.

"You didn't intend to hurt anyone?" I pressed on.

"No!" Brabant exclaimed, with the sincerity of a child proclaiming his innocence but caught red-handed by a storekeeper, nonetheless.

"This was breakfast time, and you didn't figure a member of the public would get in the way?" I was persistent.

He shrugged his shoulders

"What was the gun for?" I inquired.

"What do you think?" He looked as smug as any man who is seasoned by years of prosecutorial cross-examination. The witness stand was not a foreign place for him.

"Well, you told us at the last hearing and Commissioner, for the record I am referring to the Inmate's testimony in the transcript of January 23, 2001,

'People respect a man with a gun.'

That's why you brought it, right? To get respect?"

"Right," Brabant barked.

"Fear?" I continued.

"Yep." Brabant constricted his face to the point where you could see the outline of a vein running across his right temple. His face was red.

"And not to hurt anyone?" I asked, in disbelief. "Nope. Never have." Brabant answered mechanically.

"So, why was the gun loaded?" I inquired, with the innocence of a child asking his mother where babies come from.

Brabant thought profoundly upon this question. "I dunno."

Dennis Jones than proceeded to pick apart Brabant's performance in prison. He focused on the psych report, which showed that Brabant presented himself to staff psychiatrists as a model prisoner with a stable outlook. If you read in between the lines, it was clear that his demeanor masked a completely different individual. And so thought the shrinks, who found that he continued to evidence the clinical symptoms of a sociopath. Ms. Tarasoff was deft at pointing out why. At 10, Brabant had come home from school to find his father hanging from a ceiling beam. He had made the rounds of foster homes for next four years, and almost made it to adulthood in the quasi-custody of child protective services if he hadn't been raped by his foster brother when he was fourteen. He chose to be housed at the California Youth Authority instead. A series of violent felony crimes had been his passport.

Fourteen years later, Mr. Brabant stared at us stone-faced. He was still young enough to captain one of the prison's football teams, as well as govern as the self-appointed leader of the local Aryan Brotherhood. He said in his defense, "I'll say it again.

I am sorry. I have changed. I've paid the price. I don't know why I have to do so much time on this. I have paid the price. I think I've done the punishment. No one died here."

I made a few cogent closing remarks, pointing out that the absence of dead bodies was a stroke of pure luck. Perhaps I was still in sordid contemplation of the cover of a *Time* magazine, which about twenty years ago had displayed a young boy sprawled in a pool of blood next to the spinning wheel of an overturned bike in front of a place in San Diego. Golden arches can be seen in the background.

I didn't mention the incident; it was enough that Brabant's hollow apologies and remorseless facade hung in the air like a soliloquy of bad method acting. It was his hunter's eyes that gave him away.

Parole was denied for two years. He was led out of the room without saying a word, though I imagined the stream of epithets that were swirling around in his head. Once the door had closed, Tarasoff remarked sarcastically, "Well, that was a real nail-biter."

The commissioners smiled.

We were free for the rest of the day. I took the top down on my convertible and headed to the open market in San Luis Obispo, only fifteen minutes away. It occurred every Thursday night, which was one of the rewards of doing lifers on the Central Coast.

I parked my car alongside a curb in lot and made the walk down Higuera Street, where crowds meandered up the cordoned off street, purchased fresh produce from countless booths, and lined up occasionally for tasty barbecue cooked on huge grills by local taverns. There were bundles of fresh basil, cartons of strawberries and blueberries, baskets of large fleshy tomatoes, fresh rosemary bread and the occasional children's clown blowing up animal balloons or the young soloist playing the flute or the sax. You could buy a three-pound bag of roasted peanuts for a buck and munch on them while browsing the crafts offered up by local artisans and muse at the relative simplicity of life outside of the usual metropolitan sprawl of both ends of the State of California.

Children and adults danced spontaneously in the street to the rock 'n roll tunes of a small band playing on a street corner. I purchased a chicken leg dripping with barbecue sauce and wandered off with a bag of groceries to the Mission, which at seven o'clock was already cloaked in the orange glow of the sunset. The streetlights cast shadows across the stream that cut a swath through the center of town. I traversed a short footbridge and made my way to the streambed where I unexpectedly interrupted an embrace between two women holding each other under the parapets of the bridge.

People were having dinner on the restaurant terraces that twinkled in candlelight above the riverbed, and you could hear the chatter of lively couples enjoying the view over a glass of wine. Other than the voices in the distance, the only sound came from the water in the brook that quietly gurgled its way to the sea. I mused that at some point it had to run past the California Men's Colony. I completed my annual pilgrimage by climbing up the mission's steps, and tossing a coin into the fountain that was bordered by a statue of a young boy.

I drove back to my hotel in Morro Bay and passed the Colony on the right. A half moon shone through the clouds, and the hum of my sports car rumbled in the quiet night. To my left the ridge of the Montana De Oro had sprouted like the humps of a dinosaur tail, disappearing for some distance in a forest of eucalyptus. The air was still.

I went to sleep in my comfortable bed surrounded by all the amenities that a four star hotel with charm might provide. A 32-inch screen, a liquor cabinet, a small desk, and my own personal outdoor hot tub encircled by a balcony. I snoozed for a moment and considered that elsewhere in the town there were overweight parole officers in satin pajamas watching the late news, couples sleeping on old mattresses in trailer homes, and children dreaming on bunk beds in modest subdivisions. I surmised that at the Colony the inmates slept on army cots with inch thick mattresses and stared at the imperfections in the ceiling before they fell asleep.

I woke up on Friday morning with the comfort of knowing I would be finished early and be able to play in wine country for the rest of the weekend. The last case was the oldest, and perhaps the most brutal. In 1981, George Gutierrez had gotten himself into a fight in a bar in Silver Lake. The police report made it sound like a Latino dive where the only good thing was the Patron Tequila they served up at the counter that accompanied small dime size packets of cocaine that were bought and sold like packs of cigarettes. It was unclear how the melee began, other than the way they usually do in bars. Someone's thin-skinned ego, someone's sense of machismo, the honor of someone's mother had been offended and there would be hell to pay. Gutierrez was neither the initiator nor the ultimate victim, but he was the one who chose to kill that night. Gutierrez' drinking buddy, one Jaime, grabbed the victim, who was presumably the source of the insult, and threw him into the jukebox. The victim's friend then came to his defense, and like the last domino in a chain reaction, Mr. Gutierrez, with his three hundred pound stature, had pummeled the victim into a state of unconsciousness with his bare fists. They pulled the victim off the floor and threw him into the trunk of a Chevy Impala like a sack of potatoes. They then parked the car near MacArthur Park, a local dumping ground for people that have come to a violent end. There, the victim was pulled out of the trunk, and literally discarded behind some bushes like an old mattress. He was still breathing, albeit coughing up blood. Gutierrez' cohort egged Gutierrez to finish the guy off, so Gutierrez crushed the man's face in with a bumper jack.

We know this from the imprints that were left on what remains of the face and the matter that was found on the bumper jack stand when the abandoned car was discovered in a ditch.

Salton reviewed the offense, for which Gutierrez had received a 16-year to life sentence in 1981. It was a second degree murder, without the premeditation of a first, but calculated with an additional year because a deadly weapon, other than Mr. Gutierrez' bare hands, had inflicted the fatal wound. Commissioner Salton looked pensively at Gutierrez, who was now nearing sixty years of age, and sat before us with his cuffed hands resting on his belly, with an aura of dignity. He was portly, the way a grandfather is. The tried and true *what do you have to say for yourself?* hung like an implied platitude in the accusing stares.

Gutierrez looked meekly around. In a husky voice he started slowly. "I was a lost soul when this happened. The day at the bar was like lots of other times. I couldn't control my anger. It took very little for me to lose it in those days. A little blow, a shot or two, I was just out of control. The guy pissed me off, and the next thing I knew I was on top of him. I beat the crap out of him, and we were just going to go lay him somewhere. Someone had called the cops."

"So you thought you'd put him to bed in a park? I mean, sir, you not only beat him within an inch of his life, but you drove somewhere, and took him out of your car, and then inflicted the final coup de grace." Salton said the French word *grace* like many Americans are prone to say: *gras* with a silent "*s*," like *pate de foie gras*.

Gutierrez responded respectfully with a nod. You couldn't get around the fact that some thought and motor skills had gone into the victim's untimely demise. He wasn't left to die in the park; he was left to rot there. I was sick of hearing about lost souls wielding bumper jacks

"Counsel?" Salton pointed in my direction

"Yes, just a few questions, Commissioner."

I was waving an old parole transcript." Mr. Gutierrez, do you feel remorse for this crime?"

Mr. Gutierrez said unwaveringly. "If I could have changed the way I was. If I could do it allover again. I am not the same person today as I was then."

"But you still took a bumper jack to a helpless man's face and ..." I wasn't shy about being graphic.

"Objection!" Tarasoff seemed to have been saving all her fury for this one inmate.

"We are not here to retry this man! If we were to do this every time, no man would ever get a parole date, not in a hundred years! Can we move on to something relevant here instead of having counsel here re-enact the facts like a bad theatre scene?"

"Counsel, we need to give the Deputy D.A. some opportunity to remind us of the offense." Commissioner Salton played a good referee.

"Yeah, ya know, enough already." I could hear the Harley woman talking in her native backcountry tongue. "This man has been in for twenty three years for a crime he committed when he was a different man. Look at the psych reports. Look at the BPT summaries; there isn't a single violation!"

It was true. His record was unblemished. Not one food fight, not one can of pruno, not one wrong look. His prison conduct reminded me of the youths I had seen serving time in juvenile camp in the mountains. They were as disciplined as Marines marching in single file, sitting in rows, barking military orders, and soberly learning trades. They would be then released back to their gang and drug infested neighborhoods until the next time they were caught stealing a car or committing a drive by. The young commanders in their neat fatigues were regular guests of the institution.

"Anything else?" Commissioner Salton smiled at me.

"Would the panel please inquire of Mr. Gutierrez why it was that his rage did not subside once he had driven for fifteen minutes to a city park where he then chose to finish off this helpless victim with a bumper jack?" I remembered to follow the proper format.

Mr. Gutierrez spoke up rebelliously. "I never used no jack, I don't know where that came from. We just left him there bleeding. No one used no jack."

I held a telling photograph of the victim's remains in my hand. It depicted the face of the victim, mangled beyond recognition. "At the previous hearing, this autopsy photograph was introduced." Salton waved me away. He had apparently made up his mind.

Salton looked at Commissioner Jones. But before Jones could begin recounting the minutiae of psychobabble contained in two decades of psychologists wringing their hands, Gutierrez spoke up.

"If I could say something. You know, I don't know what the prison shrinks have to say this time. I can't think of anything new to tell you. You're gonna do what you are gonna do. It's just . . . I am an old man. I have got a new grandbaby. Two. One was born in June. And. . . ." His voice began to break. "I want to hold her. I want to be with my family. I can help my son. He needs me to come back and be a dad for once. He needs my help. I can do things out there." Commissioner Salton replied, "You have been a model prisoner. The switch has been off. How do we know it won't be flipped on again when you get out?" Mr. Gutierrez retained his dignity. "I have grown into a man. Before I was a lost soul."

"Why were you a lost soul, Mr. Gutierrez?" Salton sat stonily facing the inmate.

"Because when I was sixteen I was standing next to my baby brother… my dear baby brother. In our front yard . Two inches away. We were talking. And I heard some shots from somewhere. And then…there he was dead at my feet."

"Someone shot my baby brother dead as he stood there right next to me." Mr. Gutierrez was now speaking at a whisper. "And I had this rage," Mr. Gutierrez managed to sob quietly with dignity.

We recessed for a quick snack so that Salton could formulate his findings. Through the windows, I could see the sun blazing onto the prison yard. The room with all its trappings, its security doors, its coffee machine, its seal of the State of California, its pathetic fan blowing a semblance of comfort, its officiousness repulsed me. I wondered about the constant stream of human tragedy that had visited this long dark oak table where human existence had been extended summarily in small increments for so many.

Apparently, housekeeping was slow at the California Department of Corrections.

The corpses of a dozen flies still littered the windowsill. In ten minutes we were ready to wrap up the proceedings. Commissioner Salton began.

"Mr. Gutierrez, we are going to grant you a parole date." Mr. Gutierrez looked blankly forward at the two commissioners until the realization of freedom crept into the wrinkled outlines of his face. It was as if an elixir had been injected into the body of a dead man and caused it to spring back to life. His skin went from gray to brown and his eyes, from which now streamed a torrent of tears, seemed like they had regained their vision from complete blindness. Mr. Gutierrez' lips began to quiver, his mouth made a gasp and he looked up to the ceiling, and in what can best be described as a cry of joy, he quietly exclaimed "Dio, Santo!" He swept his hand across his chest in the sign of the cross, and repeated to himself, "My grandbaby. I get to hold my grandbaby."

I sat in my government-issued chair, speechless. In all the paper trail of three days of reports, in all the routine pronouncements of facts, in all the stabs at rehabilitation, in all the recitation of the cruelty of ancient deeds, they had let someone go.

I packed my laptop, and stunned by the morning's events, I walked out and said my farewells to the Commissioners. Mary Ann Tarasoff got on her Harley and rode out onto Highway One. It would have been fitting if the sun had been setting on the ridge of the Montana De Oro.

But it was noon, and weekenders were arriving from Los Angeles. I took the top down and enjoyed the breeze as I wound my way up an asphalt road that snaked its way to a winery in the outskirts of Paso Robles. The sun was spectacular. As its rays breached the branches of the trees alongside the road, one had the impression of riding through a beautiful kaleidoscope of varying shades of light and darkness. At the vineyard I tasted every red and settled on a bottle of Syrah.

On Sunday before leaving, I went to the zoo in Atascadero. I didn't much care for it. I pretended to enjoy myself by peeking and eyeing the various exotic species, like the tayra, a type of rodent that acted much like a ferret with manners. However, the sign described them as tough little carnivores indigenous to Costa Rica known for their bite. But like most animals in zoos, they simply hid in their caves or underground tunnels. When I did spot them through the bars, I cheered them on in the hope they would come a little closer. But I was always disappointed when they quietly disappeared again back into their holes.

It was a wonder that for all the species, for all their bright emblazoned colors and shapes, this zoo, like many, had the atmosphere of a morgue. You could not hear the animals. Certainly, there were the ones that you could see, such as a sloth hanging from a fake tree branch to the lion cub eating his lunch on an island made of fiberglass surrounded by a moat. And the zoo sported flamingos, which stood there in the cement pond like marquee signs in front of a second-rate Las Vegas casino. The only thing that was missing was a placard that said, "Nickel Slots." The zoo was otherwise a place for the locals to enjoy a Sunday barbecue and to amuse their children. But, with the exception of the ubiquitous faraway cacophony of exotic birds, what struck me as odd is how quiet it was.

I drove back south down Highway 101 to the traffic that awaited me in Santa Barbara. I lit a cigarette, and propped my outstretched hand through the car window into the cool, rushing air. I listened to a Stravinsky's *Firebird* on the stereo. The notes struck me as too grandiose. I switched to the dim white noise of talk radio. The topic was sexually transmitted diseases. I turned the radio off.

Instead, I thought of Mr. Gutierrez' grandchildren. And I started to cry.

Earrings, and Other Things

After spending an educational time in the South learning about the personalities behind the portraits hanging over the federalist mantles of the Italianate villas with their verandas, I was most stricken by one thing: Earrings.

It has been a couple of years now that young people have been wearing some large orbs in their earlobes. Not hanging from, not slightly piercing through and not bobbing from them. Actually the rings are in the lobes and form giant hollow circles from which you could hang a couple of winter coats. I first saw them in Park City, Utah, worn by a young concessionaire at the ski lift. I was more intrigued than horrified, as they were the exact shape of two black checkers stuck in each earlobe dangling around like Christmas ornaments made of onyx. It was difficult to order a bloody Mary with a straight face.

At the airport in Houston I noticed a young guy walking through the terminal donning the much-improved hollow version. His lobes had been hollowed out and inserted with onion ring size Frisbees that made his ears stick out like Martian antennae. You could probably create a game of shooting a spitball through the center of both of them. It's as if the kids are mini elephants with these circular ears deliberately deformed into looking like soda pop openers.

Having not seen this fashionable form of self-immolation recently there I was wandering the river plantation home known as Middleton Place near Charleston with a kind woman of seventy or so guiding myself and a couple through the French inspired grounds typical of a plantation home in the South. She was a combination of charming and witty, her cadence relaxing from time to time on the gorgeous views of live oaks hanging over ponds encumbered with Spanish moss. She was stylish to a point, little leather booties over the ankles, a skirt of sorts belted over a protruding belly. A colorful blouse shrouded by a conservative leather jacket, to buffet the wind announced by that morning's cold front. You could have added a parasol in the right weather.

She added instead two large four-inch screws attached by nuts in her earlobes. There were delightful silver pendants hanging from each, and if your eye followed but simply stopped at the head of the bolt, you would have said, "Fine jewelry, Madam." It goes with the outfit. But from those five inches forward was a particularly industrial looking pair of screws, one inch thick that on their way, somehow pierced the skin into her earlobes, and were apparently bolted on the back. I am not a man who cares too much about details, and I understand that young people need to try new things. But what is an elderly person doing accessorizing herself to look like a makeshift Frankenstein when everything else about her screamed, "Antique"?

I wonder if now that the tattoo mantra has stuck, literally forever, that puncturing our bodies has become the next form of exhibitionism. I realize that people insert rings into their tongues, tits and penises for sexual arousal; at least you could say they are functional. And I don't want to take way from the occasional pin through the nostril or the bottom lip, or pierced earrings, because most of the time they are not so overwhelming that they take away from a person's appearance. I should say if an individual is of an ugly sort, and that can happen, it may well behoove him or her to surgically insert some device, say a small rotating blow-fan, or perhaps a miniature bonsai tree onto one or the other temple, as this may well distract the scrutiny of the exacting aesthete. The V-nose, the harelip, the cross-eyes, the chugga- chugga neckline, all the warts would be rendered oblivious.

Then the hair would come next. I think people are getting tired of it. I mean the hair. Men lose it and go bald, and now prefer just to shave it all off rather than comb the few strands across. Apparently some hair medications make the hair grow, but then they cause erectile dysfunction; there is no point in looking good if you can't perform. I suggest being bald, and joining the class action suit. You will be rich enough to buy several wigs, all from different epochs, and have children. And women…it may take a while for me to get used to bald women….But if I imagine a radiation ward, it is entirely possible that the round shape of the head would start to attract me. No curls, no lice, no stupid fashion look; just a head. Beautifully, ovally shaped. I will however have to make an exception for those like me who have the heads shaped like turnips. When I was called a jarhead once, well, I was jarred. So I suggest that those who desire to shave their heads first obtain consultants who impartially judge the situation. I would not recommend your hairdresser because they are inherently biased; they will want you to have hair so they can keep on cutting and styling it at thirty-five dollars a pop. The only problem with people all being bald is recognizing one in a crowd. I imagine we could work some sort of color code into it. It's your week; you're magenta.

And on a final note: Heels. Lately, women of the ages of twenty to fifty have seen fit to make themselves attractive by looking like deer. I am great admirer of legs, but there comes a point when putting them on four-inch f-me hoofs seems a bit too much. They prance around in these small vertical boats on their feet that spiral them to great and equally unwalkable heights. They clop more then they walk. They look like they need to be shoed by a farrier, the guy that shoes horses and adjusts everything from leg strength to lameness. Now the shoes, if that's what they must be called, are furry, two toned, spindly things that require absolute balance or a trampoline act. You see how those women walk. There is no confidence in them; it is confidence in putting one foot after another. As a man, you have evil thoughts; you either want to scream

"Fire" or invite them to play Twister. A woman's femininity is now portrayed like muscles on a man, but in this case it isn't femininity so much as it is power. Women, and I see it sparkle, in those eyes when they wear those heels, "See, look how much taller I am now, look how I prance (like you)." The men have designer suits, and the women have hoofs, and they walk armed with stilettos. How women walk with these things on, how they drive, how they operate in emergencies is a wonder. When they can really walk, they don't need these platforms. A small pump will do. They cannot learn to walk as a woman already challenged by shoes that make their feet look like they are under attack by rabbits. They first need to learn how to walk.

I do recognize the need to express one self. That is why folks tattoo themselves, pin themselves, paint themselves, puncture themselves, and dress in unique ways. We live in a vast multi populous, very commercial world where we feel lost, enveloped in an environment, which suffocates individuality. In my time, individual expression used to come from what you did, what you said, and what you wrote. Nowadays, our young folks think that the crazy tattoo on their ass or the funky earrings will identify them, without more, as harbingers of change. The problem is that you can change the way we live in an old three-piece business suit.

Quit the look and walk the walk.

The Password

It seems that in the last few years the key to checking into life as we know it is in fact a key, in fact, many keys, all secret codes and numbers and anagrams, including our mother's maiden name, or our father's birthplace, that somehow helps us access everything from our bank accounts to our frequent flyer miles. Once it seemed that the expression, "Open Sesame," unlocked the secrets to all venues. Now we are saddled with codes unique to every occasion.

If our minds were developed to have numerical photographic memories we would have no issue with these security measures. Recently I coded all of my passwords into my I-phone's m-secure application, which of course had its own password. I felt that it would be nice just to use my first name, "Marc" as the password. It certainly helped, as I was quite inclined to remember my first name. This worked for a while until one day the app left my phone for greener pastures. I am not sure where it went, and why it is the only one that disappeared. It probably traveled to Kansas to join an Android and share all my private information with a nasty wheat dealer selling religious curiosities, along with my personal X-rated email. Long story short, it can never be a short story, because registering to write anything is a long one.

Let's take an example: going to work. I am a government employee. It's not like I have a top security clearance classification; I am one of 1,000 deputy district attorneys in the crime swamp of Los Angeles. It is a horrible bureaucracy. There are webs you get entangled in everywhere the minute you set foot through the door. I just try to work and leave. This is a matter of some doing.

To check in at work, there are two things you must do. Unlike having a lovely secretary say, "Hello, Mr. Jones," with a cup of hot brewed coffee, you sit at the desk of your carrel, which is one of two which you split with your office mate, who sits on the other side of a piece of rubber board, and you log in to your computer. Luckily, at the time of this writing, I have upgraded to a closet. You log in because you are in the 9/80 program, which means longer hours and a Friday off every other week. But the first thing you do, especially if you are late, is to log on to the computer to check in through e-mail that you have arrived. My version of having arrived at the age of fifty was a bit different in conception, but that's another conversation. "Arriving" now means plugging in one employee code and one password for the computer, going to email, plugging in another password for email, all of course in upper case, and then sending a completely blank page to my secretary, (who has one of those pesky hyphenated last names), registering my check-in at work. Then I disentangle myself from this morass of cyber business, which at eight o'clock feels like the worldwide web of a spider sticking to my fingers. The cup of coffee of course is the one you brought in a broken thermos, unless you have a penchant for the two-dollar swill of the cafeteria. It is amazing you don't have to enter a code for that. Ultimately, the nice lady at the register will be eliminated eventually by a screen that scans your coffee, prices your sweet n' low and chugs out a receipt as if you were at a gas pump. But then you would have to enter your pump number.

I will miss the "Good Morning" from the Hispanic lady with whom I share a few Spanish comments that make my day. Five minutes of public business now wasted (all at the tax payer's expense), I now have to check my phone mail. And that is even more interesting. I dial the first button, hoping for a ring tone. Not finding one, I have to check my voice mail with the following codes: (1) (323) 343-4300, followed by 336699# for the messages. Then you have to listen to them, which sometimes requires an expert ability to speed delete. It always irritates me when a message is left that I haven't deleted, hanging around like yesterday's detritus. It's like a Kleenex you have blown your nose in and left on your desk and forgotten to toss.

No big deal, I suppose, except when you try to access your Charles Schwab account and find some difficulty in the password you are inputting. It is quite interesting that they imprison your money in the hopes you will forget the secret number of your key. I find that out frequent flyer carriers are the same; once you figure out the number for customer service, good luck in getting them to award you any of the miles you have conscientiously accrued over the last two years. Between blackout dates, and airport connections that require training for the Olympic 400 meter dash, they don't actually open the field until the point when you can't possibly plan your trip.

So you find that magical credit card. Oh yes, the one that gets you 20,000 miles and no interest for years. Until you are one day late on a payment and you have just accrued 24 per cent "bad person" interest for the rest of your life. There are codes of course, those secret pin numbers you hide in your suitcase on long trips in the event that some pick pocket makes off with your wallet. However, it is a bit difficult to use a pin code when the credit card it is associated with is running down Las Ramblas in Barcelona in the wallet that was once in your back pocket, but now borrowed conveniently by a thief masquerading as a flamenco ticket seller. The best the thing to do is to chase him, grab him, threaten him and wish him good hunting. That actually worked. And never dance with street flamenco ticket sellers again. They get too close to your butt.

But enough about credit cards; that is a story that someone else should write.

It is the bank that worries me next. You have all your savings in an account that you can access on line. That is a wonderful thing. I have found that you can transfer funds and avoid overdrafts in a nano second. When you cannot access your account, because of some failure of password memory, you are in trouble. No more *on line* payments; you lose your house, your credit rating, and your net-flix membership, all in one fell swoop. I am not sure what a swoop is, but a full one usually does the deal. So it was with a better of turmoil that when trying to remember which version of my name I had used to access my bank account, the computer asked me the special security question; not my Mom's maiden name, my dad's middle name, or even the name of my high school, but my favorite sports team. I was convinced someone had hijacked my account because I don't watch sports, I have no favorite sports team, and I would never have subjected myself to an inquiry of such a mysterious nature. It's like asking a blind person what their favorite film was.

So I have passwords as ordinary as combination codes for gym locks. It is frustrating to forget those codes because it reminds you that you have not been to the gym for a while. I have had a lock-hanging round in the back of my car, but the combination I recorded years ago must have been to a different one. If you don't remember the gym, and you don't have the number to your lock, that is clearly not the central problem.

Theft is the reason why we have codes. Our use of the internet and our reliance on credit cards has exposed us. You can scan a credit card, or a drivers license, and create a nice package of identifying information that belong entirely to one or two different people. You charge things for a month and then disappear. Sometimes we catch them in the process of counterfeiting a check at a bank; it is amazing the number of credit cards, driver licenses, and social security numbers you are likely to find in the car, often driven by someone who doesn't even own it. Then of course there is the laptop computer and printer you find in the fleabag motel. The suspects are registered in temporarily, replete with duplicating programs, printed blank checks that look as good as the original. However, it should be noted that sometimes those mysterious charges on our credit cards are not quite as nefarious. I recently saw a bill for 109.00 dollars, in yuans, for some unidentifiable merchandise purchased at a store in Zhaozhou, China. I wasn't in China on March 13, and have never been to Zhaozhou. I instantly thought, *Identity Theft!* I called American Express who agreed that some Chinese syndicate was up to no good and recommended I cancel my card. It is only a day after that I realized, though I had not been to China recently, my internet had. I had ordered hair growth medication from a mysterious source, and was using it with the results that were no less memorable then when ordering it through my physician. *Mea Culpa!*

We used to lose keys like we forget passwords. We could name our children at birth with secret unchanging nicknames that they could always use and remember. They of course would have to have both lower and upper case lettering and numerical and non-numerical symbols, which might be hugely difficult to pronounce. But once pronounced the secret would be out and all those not to be trusted would hear the name, and secretly deploy it to empty your children's trust accounts. Perhaps you don't speak the nick-name and merely tattoo it for life on their bare bottoms like a cattle brand. Unfortunately, they would have to be constantly contorting and exposing themselves in public to access the oft-forgotten name, but a small mirror and a beach towel might do the trick.

The options for a solution seem simple at first, yet each has its own drawbacks. Our modern day, "Open, Sesame," could be something as simple as a voiceprint where the computers or cell phones instantly recognize our unique voices. However, the accuracy may be limited for those experiencing bouts of laryngitis, the common cold, or the change of the male voice during puberty. It would seem unfortunate to saddle these innocent folks with being locked out from their bank accounts and voicemail. I understand the retina is also unique, and that eye prints could conceivably be the way devices verify our identity. However, I can hardly fathom people putting their eyeballs to their computer screens or handsets to break into their cyber worlds. It is bad enough seeing people looking down at their cell phones with the intensity of a squirrel examining an acorn.

In the end, I hope one day our fingerprints become our passwords. They have arches, loops and whorls. They are unique. Even fraternal twins don't share them. We will never have to remember our birth dates, our own carelessly named acronyms, the correct spelling of our mother's hometown. All we will have to do is place our thumb on the computer screen and it will read that we truly are who we say we are. I am sure they are working on that. Absent someone removing someone's fingertips in a mayhem-murder to use them to defraud the finger owner, I think that manner would be fool proof. If the robber of my identity removes my fingers, than damn well, just kill me because I can't operate without my hands. Good luck on that count. I will no longer be living, and you will be hounded by the finger homicide detectives until you fess up.

Naturally, we would not need codes if we trusted each other. We would not need codes because we would have no interest in breaking into the messages on someone's dating site or pretending to slander someone with emails that originate from our own i.p. address. We would not insist on a comfortable distance between ourselves at ATM's and the lines behind us. Our distrust of each other has fostered a sizable cottage industry of code crackers and computer techs. This was the origin of the house and automobile key. In the end our lives become our own personal Ft. Knox, much the way we cloister ourselves and our private lives from the intrusion of the curious or greedy.

I would personally prefer to revert to the caveman era of cash-filled mattresses and mysterious boxes buried deep in the woods. A problem is however presented with the pitfalls of overgrowth and environmental change. One man was recently charged with destroying an entire hillside in search of $25,000 in cash that he had buried in the forest of another age, some two decades before, surprised at how much the topography no longer matched what he remembered.

There really is no quick solution, other than risking the loss of your fingertips, or setting explosives that detonate when a mock-code is inputted. Perhaps not the safest solution, but one that would bring the greatest satisfaction.

LOL

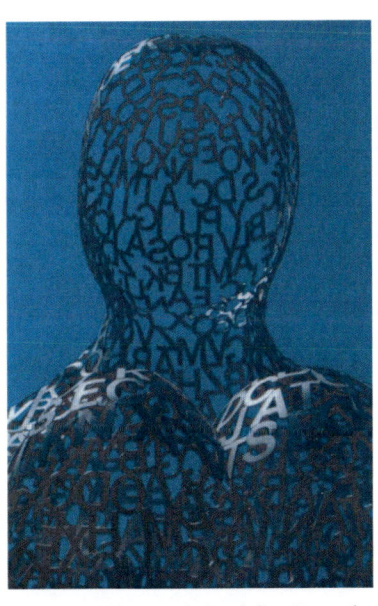

It must've been on *FB* (Facebook) that I first encountered the *LOL* anagram. Then, there were numerous texts on my cell phone where I found myself deciphering what *LOL* meant. It was apparently the newest addition to our public lexicon of abbreviated communication, but for the life of me, even with the happy face, I could not figure out what it meant. I was brought up in the days of *Groovey!* and *Far Out!* and there was always something new, like "gnarly," which described a great day on the surf or a gangrenous condition to someone's ingrown toenail. There was *dude* and *check this out* and *was sup?* all which were easily explainable. But then the abbreviations took hold. This was the result of texting. Even before, when I had moved to California in 1988, the abbreviation lingo was already on its way. You would hear about a friend who got a 502 on PCH in RB. That meant he was arrested for driving under the influence on Pacific Coast Highway in Redondo Beach on his regular day off. LOL is certainly not offensive, but one does wonder about its origins. Does someone just text his way of saying "This is funny" and almost within six months everyone is doing it? *LOL* is not what I originally thought it was: lots of luck, lots of laughs, love my old laptop. It was *Laugh Out Loud,* but I don't feel compelled to do so just because these nice little texts come my way. I am not a huge laugher, unless something is hugely absurd, so when someone says "He is kind of an odd duck, *"LOL,"* I am more contemplating what a strange duck does rather than laughing at a good joke. I am thinking you could get away with telling a woman she is a slut. If you throw LOL into the equation it softens the blow. Then of course, *it's all good.*

How can anything be 'all good?' It sounds like a pancake caked in the finest Maple syrup. Six Israelis were killed in a tour bus in Bulgaria, Syria is in a civil war, the Euro is collapsing, a kid with an arsenal shot and killed 12 people at the premiere of *Batman* and someone has the temerity to say, *it's all good.* It is never *all good.*

In spite of things not being so good, there are a number of folks that are *Good to go.*

At the risk of being brash, if someone says *good to go* to me, I am thinking of a to go pizza with onions and anchovies. It's cheeky, and cheesy, because the expression is capable of so many other meanings. For instance, a murderer arrives in his car at his killing zone. He has his getaway planned, his gun loaded, and the general idea of how he is going to off someone. He has brought water for the drive. Maybe a submarine sandwich. He is *good to go.* It would have been nice to just say, "I am ready."

I realize that texting complete sentences is difficult, so reading abbreviations has now called for a new dictionary of sorts. Also, if you scout the world of adult classifieds, you will need to know what *FWB, DDF* and *HWP* mean. Especially if you can host, *FWB,* or friends with benefits, means a noncommittal relationship where you go out you see movies, you have breakfast all, "Dutch treat," and then she gives you a blowjob, or a *BJ,* for many years part of our vocabulary. I can't imagine a soldier sitting on the frontline in World War II sending a note, an actual letter, back to the personals section of his hometown paper in Peoria, requesting a "Friend with Benefits." But then again, if you liked portly women, you would have described them politely as "Rubanesque" as opposed to today's *BBW,* the equally tender expression for "Big Beautiful Woman." However, that would hardly titillate the man in search of someone who was *HWP,* the signifier for "Height and Weight Proportionate." It would help things tremendously if you were *VGL,* even though very good looks tend to be in the eye of the beholder, especially by the one beholding his own image in a bathroom mirror. It might even help if you shared the same interests, like being *420 friendly,* which means being an enthusiastic pot smoker. Why 420? It is when kids usually get off the high school bus after a day of school. Homework doesn't appear to be the first order of business.

Even the older generation of baby boomers prides itself on their ability to communicate in code with texts and FB blurbs. *BTW, R U free 2nite? TTYS.* "By the way, are you free tonight? Talk to you soon." But sometimes they trip, and not just on abbreviations. They trip because unlike when the Yellow Pages are involved, their fingers cannot do the walking. I was reminded of the man who declared to his fiancé that he was waiting for her in his Dad's condom. Condo, silly. His girlfriend reportedly texted back *WTF?* (What the fuck?). I was mortified to find a court referee spouting on FB the comment *WTF?* She is a bench officer working with juveniles. And she quotes the abbreviation of "Fuck" on an internet site for all to see. What the fuck? How about something more like: "What's up with that?" And then of course she was complaining about a restaurant. All I can say is *OMG!*, the, "Oh my God," declarative holdover from valley girl speak, whose anagram is texted millions of times a minute on the world's cell phones. I'm getting married. *OMG!* I am going to prison. *OMG!* My ex just called me. *OMG!* Syria rebels take over Damascus. WHO? Lately *cool* has been replaced by *nice,* and *sweet.* Just like *cool,* they are monosyllabic outbursts that mirror our inability to discern and describe specific attributes of a situation. An Olympic medal for the pole vault and winning the Nobel in Literature are both *cool,* and *nice!* and *sweet!* But when repeated with such automation one tends to forget other more descriptive compliments, which involve mouthing several words: "Victory is sweet!" and, "What a nice accomplishment!" or the more sober, "such sweet revenge!" This however requires verbal calisthenics that apparently are above our capacities. The interesting thing is that *nice* is a double-edged expression that is often used sarcastically instead. In a supermarket, a woman's enthusiastic discussion on a cell-phone in a supermarket about a vaginal yeast infection may well get that retort from an eavesdropping customer, especially in the vegetable aisle. At least satire hasn't been lost on the population, though a cold verbal skewering by a wordsmith, the expression *Nice!* is not. If *Nice!* sometimes means *gross!,* then *bad* and *sick* have also flipped meanings. A person recently complimented me on a mahogany chest I made by blurting out how *sick* it was. "That is so sick!" I asked him to *shut up!,* and be *nice,* at which point he told me that it was an underhanded compliment, much like in previous years *bad* had meant "Out of this world!" I thanked him and walked him to the front door.

Speaking of *Shut up!* This mark of great surprise has now started replacing *Get Out!* and *No fucking way! (nfw!)*. The first two seemed to realistically allow the speaker to describe the tragic train accident, even if it was unpleasant. The new version of *Shut Up!* implies that we really don't want to hear about it, as it might disturb our outlook for a sunny and otherwise *awesome* afternoon. When men start using this expression, they really should consider another one, *ew!* (a sort of female *yuck!*), and then take up cross-dressing.

Incredulity is always the mark of a person who thinks they are too intelligent to have the wool pulled over their eyes, so the egotistical *Really???* And *Ya' think?* find their place.

Whereas *Give me a break* stills seemed to allow for the possibility of negotiation, *Really???* is reserved for the tall tale told by a pathological liar who is not worthy of having a single word believed. It is said in a nasal fashion, which slopes to a high note. It calls into mimicry millionaires who can't pay their taxes and cocaine users that inexplicably can't sleep.

The more juvenile expression, *Ya' think?* tends to ridicule someone for saying the obvious. It is thirty degrees below outside, a blizzard has frozen traffic to a standstill and the heater in your car doesn't work. On top of that, you left your parka at home. Someone exclaims, "It's cold!" That is where the obtuse recitation of the obvious finds its just deserts in your retort, *Ya' think?*

I suppose our language changes and incorporates new idioms to the point where words and expressions such as "googling" are now the latest entries in Webster's Dictionary's newest edition. Most of the time our expressions are innocent enough and simply connote a different way of saying something harmless. But sometimes the expressions mask a complete cultural absence of the ability to communicate that was the hallmark of the British. When the phone call is replaced by the text message, and language has become a question of signs, then the depth and subtlety of what we express is completely lost. The written word has disappeared along with our handwritten letters, and our reading is more confined to grabbing headlines than reading literature. Our courtrooms and boardrooms are no longer the bastions of persuasive oration but locales for dry, sometimes clever, PowerPoint presentations.

In the end, it isn't all good. But then our Aussie friends might politely say, upon examining the American commercialization of language, the small palliative: *No worries.*

This is the only one that I like. It is accepting of all circumstance, and much lighter than the heavy and overburdened, *no problem!* Problems are thunderous, but worries are small capillaries of issues that cause bigger problems. If there are no worries, then that is a good start.

To Hell with Sir

I must have been 29 years of age when I found myself being seriously "sirred" for the first time. He was a young bagger of groceries at Lucky's, an L.A. supermarket, and he obsequiously asked if I would like some help to my car. It was followed by, "Sir." It was odd, respectful, and entirely inappropriate for me, a single man-boy who had spent the last night drinking a wee to much scotch at a happy hour of drunken friends. I was neither a family man, a homeowner, builder of charities, nor a CEO of corporations. I was brought up to "sir" people who had grey hair around their temples, swarms of young children at their ankles, and seasoned wrinkles in their tanned faces that commanded respect and authority. I couldn't understand why a bleary-eyed young deputy district attorney had been misaligned with this older category of gentlemen. There was nothing wrong with the sirs of my generation, other than that I found them to be *plain vanilla* boring, hamstrung and stressed with problems bigger than I could imagine. They were the types that had a billfold of credit cards, a BMW sitting in waiting, a nag of a housewife, two lapdogs and bills out the nose. They hired and fired people, made decisions affecting our environment and calculated profits based on spreadsheets; they came home to a nanny who had overstepped her bounds and decided on which summer camp to send their children so he and his wife could re-ignite their romance on some Fuji paradise without the thought of all those irritating responsibilities.

"Sir," was my father, not me. I was dude, bud, you, guy, young man, but *never* sir. I refused to accept that my hairline had started receding and that for several years all that sun had started putting a few years on my face. I had wrinkle lines and when I looked at myself in those mirrors at Macy's I cringed at the sight of the bald spot emerging like a crater the back of my head. There came a time when I averted looking at my head when checking to see whether a suit fit in the merciless glare of the tripartite mirror. Then you can see not only all sides of your pockmarked face but god forbid the back of your head which had started looking liked the planet Saturn with its rings, except the rings were strings of your hair that tried stoically to cover up the skin of your exposed scalp.

As time went by I was subjected so much to the unwanted title, "Sir," that I went on all sorts of hair medications and started working out like a fiend. By forty five I was in much better shape than most of my contemporaries, but today, again, muscular, tanned, and with a new $65.00 subtle dye job of salt and pepper, I bumped into a young man as I was stepping off the abdominal machine and he responded automatically, "Sorry, sir." There is a time when it is amusing, and there is a time when it truly hurts.

Alright, so with life expectancy going up, I am told, and simultaneously emboldened by the idea that 45 is the new 35. Yeah, right. Sir is *still* sir. It is old, respectful, and done. You feel like a turkey that has now been cooked, carved, white meat there, and dark meat here. A nice browned drumstick, coarse skin and cooked to the bone. It would be more satisfying to be considered done if you had the kids, the wife, and the business trips. And though I do own a home, and was once the captain of a District Attorney satellite office of ne'er-do-wells, sort of like the mad king of Luxembourg, I was never fond of being a patriarch of idiots.

"Sir," is not quite like being the coach of a football team. In fact, it is more like being the caretaker in a mental ward occupied by older sirs and older ladies stricken with maladies of both the physical and mental variety.

Still, for all the bike riding, swimming, joking, drinking, and joie de vivre that I have, I am still relegated to the Land of Sirs, a place far above and far away, and very lonely for a man who is not and would never pretend to be a sir. It is a place for cigars and snifters, goatees and walking canes, four door family sedans and a bag of golf clubs. Sirs do not play games, they do not perform pranks, they do not laugh at themselves, they do not act in plays or take on new hobbies. They are deadly serious specimens with up curled lips, fishlike stares from eyes squinting at a slant through a pince-nez, and hunched posture. They don't so much dance as waltz, sing as hum, and yell as groan.

On a bus, a Sir does not stand for the elderly to sit as that is already the case. A man opens the door for others including the weak and disabled; but a Sir walks with a constant red carpet launched before him, doors opened by well-wishers beseeching the Sir with well-meaning after-you's. When a person of about my age attempts to do that, there is usually a stalemate and little movement lest one Sir insult the other by killing him with courtesy and shooing him in first, as if to say, "Please old, man, let me open this heavy door for you." These Proofrock-baiting specimens have at least stopped exclaiming, "Age before beauty," as that unfortunately is no longer spoken with irony.

It is interesting to think that for years youth toils so hard to earn respect and when it finally finds it, it is clutched once again by an inescapable desire to return to the wild. Youth has promise, potential, hope, opportunity, ambitions; the Sir has his regrets, property, memoirs, medications, health benefits and a dachshund or terrier to shadow him. There is a reason why the phrase midlife crisis exists, and every respectful "sir" that is uttered by the obsequious passersby only heightens the apex of this existential malaise. That is the time when men file for divorce, give up custody of their children, engage in motocross, and decide to climb Mount Everest. It is a sad and fleeting scenario, for having once abandoned ship, the Sir finds himself afloat in a morass of even bigger ambiguity without so much as the base of an iceberg to hold onto. It is cold out there for the Sir who has outlived the welcome mat of adventure and only looks like a clown trying to buy back his time of youth.

"Hey, old man, maybe you need to slow down!" Such was the affectionate remark made by the teenage driver of a sports car who took the time to stop and laugh at the spill I had taken on my ten speed while negotiating a turn. That the turn was on a sidewalk and the fall caused by a fire hydrant should not have been relevant. It could have just as easily occurred on a 50-mile bike ride that I do annually colliding perhaps with another colorfully spandex-wearing Olympic biker in the beautiful wine country of the Central Coast. However, this young man probably sported a beer belly as big as a Buddha's that would have kept him from mounting a bicycle, not to mention riding one. And the old Trans Am he drove was no doubt compensation for physical inadequacies of another sort. But once again, with his pimply faced smirk he was among the member of that cabal of young ignoramuses who relish sinking their poisonous fangs into your ego with the enthusiasm of vipers, just to sink in the reminder of that big neon clock ticking thunderously away.

A Sir thinks not so much of the bright future of easily conquered obstacles but looks back in melancholy on a past of missed opportunities. Occasionally you smile at your accomplishments. For instance while swimming laps in the YMCA pool, I routinely count the countries I have visited as if it was some sort of mantra. A Sir occupies himself with these small petty lists, as a way to exercise his memory, not his abs. In spite of my 36 laps, I keep on forgetting that I spent three weeks in Turkey.

I am lately become annoyed that I am shrinking. It appears that I have lost three quarters of an inch in height in the last two years. I sometimes feel like I am merging with the floor. If this keeps up, I'll become so small that that I might even appear less than respectable. I am afraid I may become a small piece of the floor, like one flat mosaic tile mixed in with the terracotta accents of someone's limestone kitchen floor. That is the worse kind of Sir, the one you have to peer down at to finally notice. A person of inconsequential proportions hardly commands respect.

I believe it is important to act courteously to members of the public and your colleagues and acquaintances. If you act chivalrous in your relationships with women or act fairly and professionally with your male contemporaries then you are considered to be a true gentleman. That is a perfectly acceptable compliment. However, when a woman standing behind you in the supermarket line says sharply to her six year old "Don't bother the gentleman, honey," then it has a different meaning.

You have just been 'sirred' in the slyest fashion, and treated like a fragile relic who might be disturbed by the horseplay of a young child.

It would occasionally be nice to be called by my first name. It is simple monosyllabic "Marc," but apparently much too informal for a man of graying demeanor and wrinkly features. Thus, "sir," like, "monsieur," or, "señor," or, "herr" is the moniker that comes to the mind of the arrogant young who are ready to sweep you away into the dustbin of human existence. I would like to arm wrestle them all, cheeky, undeveloped bastards.

If I am going to be called, "sir," then it may as well be with the fanfare of the British Title awarded to people like Sir Richard Burton or Sir Anthony Hopkins. I wonder how many Oscars you have to win, or how present you have to be in the public imagination, to be so honorably knighted. Do they actually have a committee akin to the one that awards the Nobel in Stockholm, where people of varied charitable and artistic backgrounds are nominated to be 'sirred' or 'damed'? If you are married does your spouse carry a similar title, such as a duchess would who is married to a duke, or is she relegated to being a simple Ms. that is overshadowed by the grandiloquent Sir that is her spouse. When introducing them to a grand ball at the top of a staircase, do they say Sir Robert Thornton and Mrs. Thornton? You see, she hasn't done anything to be a dame other than being married to a Sir, so I suppose she inherits no title.

Unfortunately, being called sir in the courtroom, office corridor or supermarket line carries no touch of respect for nobility; it is merely a sign of deference to the aged and diseased that are on their way to quick disintegration.

I am often tempted to counter the sir insult with an equally demeaning address. For instance, "May I borrow your pen, sir?" can certainly be followed by the flippant retort, "certainly, son," or "most definitely, miss." I would often precede this with a frown that suggests that children should be seen and not heard, but perhaps a patronizing pat on the head would suffice. The titles, "Youngster", "Baby," "Kiddo", and "Me laddie" (with an Irish twang) would certainly seem to get the point across as well. I once had a boss who managed to bring the self-esteem of her fully grown adult employees down several notches by using the African-American moniker, "that chile". Every attack of verbal ageism has its complimentary youthist putdown. And every gesture of patronizing unctuousness, such as opening a door for a Sir, can be countered with offering your bus seat to a teenager who may have a problem with his balance depending on what he has been smoking.

The passage of time and the death march of middle age are difficult enough to deal with without having to be reminded of your lost youth by the insulting title *Sir*. Your hairline recedes, your posture wilts, and your memory fades. An honest look in the mirror or the use of those ubiquitous reading glasses when glancing at a restaurant menu send you plummeting into the depths of depression. So it would respectful to be glamorized by an occasional "Dude", "Man," or casual, "Buddy." "Boss," "Mr. President," and, "Your Majesty," are perfectly appropriate and resound much more with true respect and awe than a mealy mouthed, "Sir," which merely camouflages the arrogance of the young and inexperienced.

I was in court the other day settling my daily array of felony cases where I work as a calendar deputy district attorney. This is a far cry from the battlefield of tactics and egos where freedom is lost and won in the realm of the criminal trial. My job is to dispose of progress reports, probation violations, proof of community service along with making offers to defense counsel in serious cases. After twenty-five years of hearing excuses, it is natural for a person in my shoes to become somewhat jaded by the universal lack of accountability present in a majority of those that are accused of crime. One thing that particularly riles me are those that do not show up in court. It is not a hair appointment, a date, a tee time. You are out on the streets thanks to the court's indulgence, and the one thing of importance next to waking up in the morning is keeping your court date. What is even amazing to me is that many of these derelict defendants don't even see fit to call the court to explain why they are late or can't show up. Most people have the decency at least to cancel restaurant reservations, just out of courtesy.

One day a young surfer type dragged himself in around ten in the morning on one of these "bench warrant walk-ins". He had failed to show up two and half months before and apparently had heard there was a warrant out for his arrest. I am surprised this would have come as a revelation, considering our system of justice is not entirely voluntary. He sported a scruffy beard, his hair stood up straight on his head, and tattoos mapped both of his arms. When the court took note of him, the judge alerted the bailiff to get ready to place the man in custody. The public defender spoke briefly to the defendant and asked him to sit down and wait.

The court called the case, and with the impatience of an executioner, demanded to know why the man had missed his court date.

The attorney first spoke for him. "Your honor, Mr. Blevins is very sorry for missing his court date. He said that he lost the paper his lawyer gave him and confused the dates."

"Where is the slip of a paper his attorney gave him with the wrong date?" The court inquired.

I couldn't wait to hear how his dog had eaten it.

"He says he lost it at the homeless shelter he was staying at when he got robbed."

"Which shelter is that?"

The man shifted, and exclaimed," Judge, I forgot. It's like over there on Aviation." He waved in an easterly direction.

The court knew as we all did, that Aviation was a residential thoroughfare where shelters had been banished by the taxpayers. The court was fuming.

"First of all, Mr. Blevins. You don't refer to me as 'Judge.' My title is 'Your Honor.'"

Mr. Blevins retorted. "Got it."

"Got it, Sir." The judge put additional emphasis on "sir." The court liked to consider itself as the judicial version of boot camp.

Mr. Blevins mimicked, "Sir!" with a little click of his heels, encased in torn sneakers without laces.

The court continued. "And why didn't you call the court when you realized you didn't have the date?"

"My aunt died and I had to take care of...." The lawyer interrupted him and told him to shut up.

"His aunt died and he had to take care of his niece." The attorney parroted him, afraid he might dig himself into a deeper hole.

The court stared at the defendant, incredulously. "Did the niece join you in the homeless shelter?"

The defense attorney stammered. "Your honor, he says she's okay now, but he has medical issues. He was bitten by a shark while surfing." I was trying to keep my eyes from glancing too obviously at the ceiling. It was a miracle I was keeping a poker face during this colloquy. The court looked to the bailiff and nodded. "Oh, we have plenty of medical care in lock-up," don't we Deputy Barrie? Ron, the bailiff, approached the defendant and you could hear the unmistakable sound of handcuffs being readied.

The defendant then spoke up. "Please Sir, I can't go in there. Sir, I can't! They will...."

The attorney spoke up. "Your honor, he says he was raped in jail. He didn't want to come to court because he was going to be sent to jail on this case."

"That's what they all say counsel. The jails are secure here." The court shook its head.

The defendant was practically apoplectic. His expression conveyed the look of fright of an impala right before a kill. While shaking all over, he looked at me with a pleading look that I will never forget.

Unrelenting, the judge announced, "Place him in custody, deputy. Set this matter for a hearing in two weeks."

Like words that had their own sense of independence, the following remark flew out of my mouth before I had a chance to block it. "Your honor, if I could be heard briefly."

The court leered at me, cognizant that I was about to upstage it.

"This defendant has no record other than the pending drug case. It was a meth case, and I would take an educated guess that Mr. Blevins is heavily addicted. Rather than place him in jail where he will get no help, and be locked up at the taxpayers' expense, perhaps we could refer him to the in-patient clinic known as 'The Lighthouse,' and have him come back with proof of counseling."

The defense attorney and the defendant stared at me in unison as if they had both been hit by the same truck. The court hesitated, with a note of exasperation. "Fine, Mr. Prosecutor. Mr. Blevins, do you understand what this means?"

"If you fail to show up and we place you in custody, you will be going straight to the joint. Do not pass go, do not collect two hundred dollars. Got it?"

"Yes, Sir." The defendant looked at the judge obediently.

"Case is continued until September 23, 2012. Next case." The court went about its business.

The defendant turned and while heading out of the courtroom stopped and looked at me.

He said with relief, "Thanks, bud."

My neck snapped around as if I had been a rattlesnake whose tail had been stepped on.

"Oh, and to you, Mr. Blevins, it isn't dude, bro, bud or mate. It is sir. Get it ?"

"Got it, Sir." The defendant gulped and left.

I suppose we all hate to be reminded by titles that we are not invincible or forever young. But titles like "sir," do not simply connote legal rank, judicial authority or parental respect.

They signify the deference to which moral judgment grounded in experience is entitled.

FICTION

Henry

I am forever fascinated by the younger generations natural aptitude for using high tech devices, but I was apparently born without the necessary genes to enable me to universalize a remote, use a wifi on a laptop (though I still call it a, 'labtop'), not to mention the touch keyboard strokes that are the gateway to writing complete sentences, or the abbreviated language of texting, particularly useful when announcing a death in the family. Thankfully, in some respects I am still old school and still prefer the art of writing with a pen in complete sentences book ended with beginnings and ends, and much prefer the spoken word, over the phone, than punching in the keys to an anagram as if I were playing piano on the very mini version of a baby grand, trying to communicate a state of being.

This being said, my friend Henry changed all that. I met him at an airport in Nice, a curt British gentleman who had a knack for tolerating my Latin outbursts of frustration with high technology. Of course more than once I found his unflappable nonchalance to near fatal car accidents to be unsettling, as I would listen to his mellifluous repetitions of road directions as if he were the computer Hal from *2001: A Space Odyssey*. My challenge became trying to ignite a fire in his belly, or to cause him some outburst of glee, such as, "Eureka! I found it," which was seldom my response to his navigation. We drove through the South of France together, to places like Cannes, Antibes, and the far-flung villages of Haute-Provence, through a Byzantine pathway of turnabouts.

Henry's voice was commanding and there was no equivocation in his suggestions like, "You know, maybe you should try this or that. Maybe this would be a better idea, but let's see…" But he did not wear shoes that put an impasse in a hike, since he did not have legs; he didn't shop incessantly, as he had no need for things; he did not experience paranoia in foreign countries, as he was used in all of them; and he did not need to constantly take pictures, as he knew I would.

The wondrous thing about Henry was that he was not going to upset the applecart about my traveling pace or the places I chose to visit; he just sat there on my dashboard and relayed a constant stream of impersonal information. Or so it was in the beginning. He did not guilt me into being too aggressive about traveling early and far. He did not fight with me over the dinner bill, and he did not protest when I had to leave him in the car as I ran to a place, usually to a bush or an alley, when my five-minute bladder gave the all-too-late warning sign. Henry didn't really care whether we saw cathedrals or cliff top villages or museums; he hardly ever got out of the car. And when he did, he was always packed away, charged up soon enough with a new set of directions. Henry was the one person I talked to the most during my two week trip in the south of France; he heard me mumble, chant dog names, scream, "What the fuck," in three languages, and felt me tossing his instrument around out of frustration with his misdirection. He was that one voice, no matter how badly recorded, my one passenger, my solitary conversation. He was my GPS.

I met Henry at Avis-Rent-A-Car. He came with a little black charger that fit into the lighter, a small screen that had some interesting graphics. I don't know what Henry looks like in person but I do know that his voice, with its perfect diction and restrained discipline, would dance circles around Tom Robbins. It reminded me of my Uncle Henry's voice, who hailed from Gibraltar. His traditions were tea, his demand etiquette, and his language was absolutely unimpeachable. I named my GPS Henry so I could kick him around a bit given that I was a Texan with a heavy Italian and French heritage.

When you have a Henry (or GPS) in your car, you make a choice; you either rely on his voice, or you rely on the maps of the Michelin guide sitting on the passenger seat. You rely on what Blanche Dubois once called the "kindness of strangers" or you rely on the reliable maps of a respectable map company that unfortunately your unassisted eyes cannot read. It is always frustrating that a stoplight turns green the minute you unfold a map. There is distance and time to finding the right page in any guide, be it Thomas or Michelin, when you are driving down a course through Nice with little misbegotten streets with no clear signs. There is a tunnel at some point, but you don't know where that point is as you are traveling along the beautiful Mediterranean from the Airport. Oh, there are folks walking the boardwalk, and you are going too fast to talk to them and when you do talk to them, in bad irritated French at a stop sign, they give the grumbled confident phrases of this or that street, and by the time you have left them, the waves in this direction or that, and unknown distances, leave you missing the secret exit once again. Henry of course was stalwart in demanding this street or that, and though the colored lines with arrows pointing on his screen were clear as day, they were so inaccurate that I found myself doing the old town in a rental car with its one way streets with four hours of sleep from my international flight. I did the grid in a perfect square four times, coming back to the Boulevard of the Americans each time with no clue as to where the actual escape route was. It came later, but Henry was not up to it then. When I finally found the tunnel much further away, and came out into the splendor of the city, I did not know where I had to go to find this little street where my hotel was at. All at once Henry blared from his position inside the windshield, "You are at your destination!"

Now how the fuck was that possible? I was in the middle of a thoroughfare bordered by a parking garage to my left and apparently Vieux Nice on my right. Small streets that became little alleys that constructed a rabbit warren of hideaways and little rivulets of walled in streets that went into the brink. Why was I at my destination in the middle of a road where people were traveling a 40 km /hr pace and there was neither a hotel's beaming marquee on either side to tell me I was correctly positioned. I however was persistent. If Henry's pleas were correct perhaps the hotel was nearby. "You are at your destination!" again made me think perhaps, just perhaps, I am not supposed to drive into a circular driveway in front of a beaming cathedral.

The GPS advised in words that seemed less impersonal, "Go quietly." This must have been some additional polite advisement added to the recording, although it was odd that the advice seemed well-suited for being parked on a cobblestone pedestrian path that went up to the cathedral steps, right in full view of the gendarmerie. Instantly, I looked in the dark street next to the church that led to the maze of walking streets that comprised Vieux Nice. There was the poor excuse for a hotel, three stories and wedged in between two cafes in a horizontal space of about 25 feet. I made my way and checked in before being redirected to a parking garage several blocks away.

The next day I drove the car to the Matisse museum, and viewed the master's works, near where he was interred. The minute I got back into the car I realized I had failed to make a restroom stop at the museum. I assumed I could just wait until I got to the hotel, but I quickly realized that the five-minute warning that my bladder had become accustomed was not going to go the full distance. But this was not the United States where there were public restrooms at every intersection gas station. The traffic was getting jammed, and the situation was becoming urgent. "Shit, I have gotta pee!" I exclaimed, squeezing my crotch and contorting myself in the ultimate discomfort.

Out of nowhere, Henry's voice beamed, "Take an immediate right. Take an immediate right." I followed the instructions blindly. "In 300 meters, turn left, and park." I wasn't sure what was happening. I looked for a container of some sort to relieve myself in the car, and dreaded the possibility of jumping out in mid-traffic and exploding on the pavement. I turned right after the turn was an empty parking space in front of a bistro. They were open, and I put on the brakes and came to a stop, the car screeching noisily. I jumped out in a cloud of dust that arose around my car, planted myself at an outside table, and caught the waiter by the elbow.

"Un Campari, s'il vous plait."

"Bien sur, monsieur," and then I sheepishly requested, "La toilette, s'il vous plait?," at which time he pointed to the corner of the bar.

Gasping, "Merci" under my breathe, I trotted to the WC and shook the front door, only to see that the placard declared, "Occupied." The bladder was on its thirty-second countdown and I looked nervously around for a nook or cranny. There was none in site, just a band of British revelers getting drunk at the bar. I looked down at my jeans, still dry, and I forced my knees together and looked like was having an attack of spasms. I heard the bathroom knob turn, and the minute so much as a crack showed in the doorway, I bolted open the door, leaving a youngster still zipping his jeans with a look of complete horror. I whisked him away, with an anglicized comment, "Charming weather, don't you think?"

I was at the head before the door had even shut. I had not a second to spare. I walked out comfortable, still dry, but definitely the cause of some hilarity at the bar. I slapped the youngster on the back, "So sorry, old Chap." Henry would have been proud. I sat down and gulped my Campari quietly, nursing a strong desire to melt into the florid wallpaper of the bistro's walls.

I got back into the car, and composed, turned on some music. An old Edith Piaf song was playing. The GPS came on with a written blurb on the video screen, and the voice of Henry declared, "You're welcome."

I retorted, "Excuse me?" I looked around my seat and outside to see who was addressing me.

"And when you say 'Chap', the 'a' is short, unless you want to sound like you're from Manchester."

"Where are you?" I was either having a nice conversation with myself or the Campari had gone straight to my head. I settled on the latter, though talking to someone else might've been nice. I had never been to Manchester.

The next morning I toured the old town and then decided to go visit the beautiful cliff top village of Eze about an hour away, perched on the Mediterranean coast. I turned the GPS on and finally felt that the disembodied voice and I were on the same page. "In 250 meters, turn right." I was worried we were speaking in European measurements, as I had no concept of what 250 meters looked like.

"And then turn left."

We turned down the beautiful stretch of Le Boulevard des Anglais, which bordered the coast. I wish Henry had simply said, "Go to the ocean." But it seemed he was on the money.

"Lovely day, isn't it?" This time it beamed directly from the GPS. How did the GPS know it was not a day of rain? It was in fact a day that the Cote D'Azur wore like a song on its sleeve; the unfolding of the massive waves on the long strip of beaches, the palm trees and maritime pines lining the grand boulevard, the cloudless sky and people bicycling along the beach. The GPS probably had a climate application.

As I drove the Renault down the coast, the video screen for the GPS displayed a long direct line that snaked along the coast to the cliff top village of Eze. Eze was named as one of the 1,000 places to see before you die in the book by that name. It was a medieval commune that had been influenced by the Phoenicians. An Egyptian cross hung in the church, and the place was renowned for its views of the Mediterranean, where it stood like an eagle's nest perched on a cliff.

A Renault goes fast, but not as fast as a Ferrari. As I turned a curve going 65 km/hr, I saw the front of a red Ferrari tagging my rear. He wasn't actually tailgating, but it was apparent he could take these curves with a little more spin. I could see a blonde woman in the front seat. All at once, the GPS, which I had already nicknamed Henry, declared, at of nowhere, "Take the first left." I assumed Henry was mistaken. The road to Eze may not have been satellite savvy. The road I was on went straight to Eze.

It was the second time that worried me. Henry announced in perfect commanding British diction with an English voice, "Take the first left!"

Only much louder. I yelled back, "Dude, chill. It's fine. We are going the right way."

I was going 65 km per hour, the Ferrari was picking up speed, and the summer was beautiful. I was holding my own. The last declaration came like a loud ultimatum. The pines were passing in a kaleidoscope of green, the sea was on my right, licking forbidding cliffs. Trapped in the format of announcements, Henry declared, "Take the first left!" So I put on the brakes, and found myself on a dirt road heading to a private vineyard. The Ferrari sped on.

When the dust stopped I asked, "What the fuck was that all about, Henry?"

No response. I reprogrammed Eze into the GPS, and I waited. Two minutes went by and it came up. I backed out and headed back down the freeway. In thirty seconds I saw the ambulance.

A Fiat's remains were in the middle of the street. The ambulance stood idle, because it appeared that no one had survived. The Fiat had apparently been passing the vehicle on its left, across the double yellow line and had caused another vehicle to veer into the rail. I parked and looked own, and some five hundred feet below the sea cliffs, I saw the Red Ferrari in the sand, upside down.

I parked on the shoulder of the road, and rested my head on the steering wheel. I couldn't cry, but my lips shuddered silently. And this time, I groaned, "Thank you."

Henry replied, "You're quite welcome." Soberly, I drove on to Eze, and parked along the street and made my way up the steps of the medieval village. There were small boutiques and tiny restaurants, but none of them had taken anything away from the magnificence of a small thirteenth century village topped by the steeples of an ancient church that looked out to the ocean below. There was a small botanical garden of succulents on the hill. I stopped for a glass of Prosecco and a slice of pate de foie gras, still in a daze. As the sun went down, I made my way back down the cobblestone paths to the car. Henry was waiting.

I got in and said, "Alright dude. Who are you?"

Henry replied in laconic rhythm, "It's time to go forward. It's time to go forward."

I left Nice the next day, pointing my way towards Cannes for the film festival. Henry was mostly silent, except when he had to shout, "The second turn at the roundabout. The fifth turn at the roundabout." I seemed to be going in circles but always picking the right turn on the circle to get me to places like Juan-Les-Pins and Antibes. By the time we had made it to Cannes I was playing, 'What's your favorite movie,' with Henry. I would say the title and his video screen would give me thumbs up or down. We disagreed on *It's a Wonderful Life*. I thought it was an affecting piece of work; Henry dismissed it as Hollywood schlock of the worst kind. He even chimed in, "When Jimmy Stewart tried to throw himself off the bridge, my only retort was 'Jump!'" When I got back o my car in Cannes, after changing in a pair of slacks, my GPS looked at me and said, "Are we having fun yet?"

I responded, "No."

I had watched the paparazzi take photos of the beautiful people on the boardwalk, watched the commoners stretch their camera straps to get a picture of Nicole Kidman coming out of the Hotel Martinez on the Boulevard de la Croisette, and sat at a bar waiting for a scotch and water and treated like I was tourist fare. This was not the Mediterranean openness that I cherished. It reminded me of watching the Oscar parade in Hollywood. I met Gilas there, a beautiful girl with green eyes and soft brown skin. She was working on her dissertation. We cozied up at the same table of a hotel bar, while the Catherine Deneuve fanatics left in exodus to get a shot. She had an interesting eastern European accent but spoke many languages.

"So why are you here alone, Marc?" An accusing finger played with the smoke from her cigarette.

"I am not alone. I have friends." I felt defensive. I didn't travel well with buddies.

"Where are they?" she cooed.

I laughed. I asked her "Where are you from?"

She pointed in the general direction of Marseilles. "My family moved here many years ago."

"Would you like to travel to the Luberon with me?" The Luberon was a beautiful part of the inland hill country of Provence illuminated by vineyards, hilltop villages, and history. It was the next stop.

"I have to be back by Saturday. I can grab a train."

"What is your name?"

"Gilas."

When she got into the front seat, I put the keys in the ignition but the car's engine wouldn't start. Gilas got out to smoke a cigarette. I looked under the hood and got back in the car.

"Who's your companion?" Henry appeared disgruntled.

"She's a woman I met at the bar of the Intercontinental."

"Where does she come from?" Henry barked unhappily.

"I don't know. Why does that matter?"

"I don't like her. She's not a proper girl for you to court."

I mimicked this last retort. The idea of courting someone had not entered my mind. "A bit too cockney, aye? Sorry Henry. But I am not interested in her pedigree." Gilas returned. I started reconnecting the battery. That didn't work.

I began to get frustrated. So I began calling Avis when the dashboard proclaimed, "Put the car in park, you imbecile."

I looked questioningly at the gears and saw that in fact the car wasn't starting because the lever was in the drive mode. I stood there speechless and in complete disbelief. I put the car in park, and immediately started the engine.

"Get us to Grasse, you prig."

"Parsley. Noun. A green. A cultivated plant with greenish yellow flowers and aromatic, often curled leaves used to flavor or garnish some foods."

"Not sprig, you dumbshit."

The GPS spat out monotonous commands that got us to the streets of Grasse, the perfume capital of Europe. There the smell of perfume and flowers wafted from the open doors of perfume shops and filled the air with scent of lilacs in bloom. I bought Gilas a sample of Chanel. Mechanically, Henry directed our route to the rugged ridges of hills known as the Luberon. Here and there country cottages and steepled town dotted the countryside, which was in bloom with rows of lavender that purpled entire hectares of land. We stopped at the Mas des Herbes Blanches, a beautiful five star farmhouse in the middle of the Luberon valley. We checked into the large corner bedroom overlooking the white washed fields and swimming pool. We dined al fresco and enjoyed a meal of pate de foie gras followed by un canard magret, which is a sort of candied duck. After dinner Gilas insisted on retiring to the room for our own version of desert. The silhouette of her supple breasts stood out in front of a window that reflected the beaten orange sun.

In the morning Henry barked orders as if he was an itinerary robot. "To see the Luberon valley clearly one must travel to…" and Henry ticked off a half a dozen cliff top villages that could not be missed: Gordes, Roussillon, Saignon, Lourmarin, Joucas, and Bonnieux. Drenched in the light of Cezanne and Van Gogh, the villages each were a trove of discovery. There were those boasting open markets spilling with local produce, while others simply lined the cobblestone streets with the eponymous boulangerie and charcuterie, where fresh baguettes and cuts of meat hanging in the storefront windows were sold to the judicious customer. I bought a selection of cheeses that rendered the interior of the rental car smelling like an n old pair of sneakers, and the GPS had a tantrum. Henry exclaimed, "You had best be eating those soon or I'll be directing you to Stalingrad. They don't have smelly food items there. What is wrong with a good soup and a chicken pot pie?"

I retorted, "They don't have food in Russia, Henry."

While driving to Roussillon, Gilas and I opened a bottle of Bordeaux to accompany the strongest goat milk cheese we could find, and of course there were breadcrumbs all over the seats. We had a simple Swiss army knife to cut the baguette, and the interior would have been a feast for pigeons. Henry did not see it that way. He made us travel pointlessly in the wrong direction for thirty miles. The car stopped at the fenced in entrance of an old forgotten vineyard and all Henry had to say, through the speaker, was "oops." Then, frustrated, I asked him what the hell he was doing, and he remained silent for a minute.

Then the disembodied voice declared, "If you want a cafeteria, go back to America." Gilas, half asleep in the front seat, asked me if this was part of the GPS program, and I simply replied, "No honey, the wine has gotten to you." Henry chuckled, though his laughs seemed to blend into the roar of the engine that started anew. Henry redirected us properly to Roussillon, with its red rock and village of half walls and vistas of old vines.

We then headed to Lourmarin, which was laid out with an extraordinary castle on its right and the village of cobblestone streets on its left. Somewhere in its ramparts was a cemetery where Albert Camus was buried. I fondled Gilas' left knee. And then I entered the word Camus into the GPS now known as Henry and it sat there and thought a moment. I could have sworn Henry was watching me. A little red light flickered. And then the voice declared, "An excellent cabernet produced in the Napa Vineyards of California."

"Thank you, Henry. I wasn't referring to Caymus." It was a well-known vineyard in California.

"Are you quite done with the wine, then? Because I cannot drive the Atlantic Ocean."

I plugged in the first name, "Albert," to see if I got more specific results.

The car activated in a certain direction between town and castle to an old field of gravestones that were not visible from the road. The Renault stopped. Gilas was yawning, "Are we there yet?"

I looked at her brown, angled face and sleepy green eyes, and wondered why such a beautiful woman could not have cared less about the gravestone of the greatest existentialist writer of the twentieth century. I got out of the car with camera in hand and walked through the cemetery.

I passed rows of gravesites, and then saw an old woman with another of about seventy planting geraniums around a cross. I asked in French if they would mind telling me where Camus was buried.

"Oh, Monsieur, sans problème. Il est là, à côté de mon mari et mon fils." I paused, for what she had said about the neighboring graves was more important than a famous writer being buried next to them. They belonged to her husband and her son. She was an iron lady who had weathered every form of tragedy, including the loss of her own son.

I replied, "Je regrette tellement pour vous." My heart went out to her.

"Oh vous savez, Monsieur, c`a été une vie tres dur." Life had been hard. She showed me the plaque that stood above the remains of one of the most thought-provoking writers of the generation before mine. Killed in a car accident at 47 and now buried next to his wife. The writer of *The Stranger* and *The Plague*. I was 48.

I looked at the grass-covered patch of ground, and paid my respects.

Henry was steaming when I got back to the car. The GPS announced in perfunctory fashion, "The bitch won't stop snoring." Indeed, Gilas was laid out in the back seat, her skirt up to her ass, a hand on the bottle of wine, sounding like the TGV train whistling through the countryside.

The next day Henry and I dropped her of at the train station in Aix-en-Provence after a nice luncheon on the Cours Mirabeau at a renowned café known as Les Deux Garçons. Gilas gorged herself on the medallions of filet mignon as if it had been her last meal. Les frites françaises were devoured in great mouthfuls. She wore a coquettish green skirt that showed her brown and tender legs. At the station we parked, and kissed. Teary, she headed to the turnstiles of the railway station. I had purchased a one-way ticket back for her. She was the still the beautiful itinerant waif that jumped from voyager to voyager, like a small backpack that you carry and nurture as long as the visit can last.

When I got back into the car, Henry's voice accusingly asked: "Marc, where is your passport?"

Henry knew where I kept it. The left rear pocket of my jeans.

It was gone.

I got out of the car and looked at Gilas in the station and she turned her head and looked at me. She quickened her pace towards the turnstiles. I ran towards her. She walked quicker, as I did. She rushed through the turnstile in her green skirt. She was agitated.

As she got through, I jumped over the turnstile and reached for her but she ran to the platform. She managed to get on the steps of the outgoing train, the leather Prada purse that I had bought for her swinging from her shoulder. But then a large man tried to enter the passenger car in front of her. As the train leapt forward, I reached for the purse strap and pulled it off her shoulder. Gilas looked back angrily. The purse hit the platform with a "thunk!" I looked inside, and recovered what was mine. The train started charging forward. The gendarme was approaching, and before he got there I threw the bag back through the passenger window into one of the compartments. I exclaimed as he approached, "Une petite histoire domestique!" He looked at the passport and wallet that I was holding, both which were mine, and looked up with seeming annoyance. He commanded, "Bougez." Move. So I got out of his hair. When I returned to the Renault, Henry was beaming.

The lights around his GPS and video screen were lit up like the Fourth of July. Red lights, dotted flashing green lights, an occasional trumpeting sound from the audio source that usually recited street directions. After the fanfare had died down, Henry said "I did tell you, didn't I?"

As I caught my breath, the door of the car still open, I replied, "Shut the fuck up, Henry."

Henry retorted, "Don't they have gypsies in the States, Marc?"

The trip to Avignon was uneventful. The Palace of the Popes and the famous half bridge across the Rhone that sent children to sing was beautiful. The Romans had a presence in Avignon, though the walls they built lie buried somewhere under the modern streets. Vestiges of the forum could still be seen, lying unassumingly near the Rue Racine and the Rue Saint-Etienne, to the west of the city. But the palace at the end of the Boulevard still stood as the greatest installation of Gothic architecture in the world. I then traveled to Villeneuve-des-Avignon, the twin city across the river. Henry was chafing, sitting in a parking garage while I took a tour bus to see this castled town. I came back impressed with my visit, particularly of the cloisters of Chartreuse du Val de Benediction. The cloisters were an impeccable square of habitation and prayer for monks, and resonated with quietude. The extravagant palaces known as livrées on the Rhone built by wealthy cardinals were grandiose.

When we drove around, Henry, now sounding like an irascible old man, began quoting Coleridge's "Rime of the Ancient Mariner," and reiterated the line, "with wings 'til death" numerous times.

We headed north to Chateauneuf du Pape, the famous wine-growing region of the Rhone valley that produces some of the most famous varietals. Chateauneuf was my absolute favorite wine; strong, fruit forward, bold, and powerful. Henry was taciturn, except for the occasional "in three hundred feet turn right." The sloped valley carpeted with rows of vines beckoned us on.

In the square of the town, a sign sported the image of a red-nosed man smiling, "Bienvenu," while holding a bottle of wine in his hand.

As I closed the car door, I heard a meek remark coming from the GPS speaker, "I want to come."

I smiled. At least one of us would remain sober.

I walked to several wine cellars and met the local winemakers. It was only 10:30 in the morning. A sweet portly lady of sixty whisked me into her cellar where the damp barrels were lined in rows. On a dimly lit wooden counter, she poured me a glass from a bottle and asked where I was from. When I said I was from Los Angeles, she assumed I was a movie star, and it took me sometime to dissuade her of that notion. She was country, and her family for generations had been making Chateauneuf du Pape wine. She poured a glass for herself, and with a "cin cin," we drank the nectar together. I wished her adieu, and she gave me the rest of the bottle, which was still half full. I tucked it in the front seat of the car and walked onwards to the Trintignant tasting room, which was supposed to be top of the line. A set of stairs descended to a well-appointed caveau. There, a young man in a red vest and bow tie introduced himself as the son of the premier Chateauneuf family of the area. He spoke with the rapid sophistication of a Parisian, and had the attitude to go with it.

Within a matter of a minutes he had roundly criticized all the middling wine growers who sold their bottles in the cellars on the square and claimed the pedigree, but claimed their bottles were not appropriately labeled, "Mise en bouteille au chateau." Though I spoke in French with him, he, unimpressed, insisted on responding in English as if to say that his English was significantly better than my French. It was not. It was true his wine was the best on the square, and sported its price accordingly. By the time I had completed four tastings, which were served in abundant half glasses of swirling purple Rhone, my head was spinning. Jean-Louis exclaimed, "It has such a nose!" I not only had smelled the delicious bouquet, I had eaten the entire floral arrangement. I order a half a case for shipment, and three spare bottles to transport in the car and consume as I saw fit. I took out my credit card and when I realized the amount was 1200.00 euros. I gasped, my eyes protruding from their sockets.

I shook my head and I began to sign. Jean-Louis, self-satisfied, and with considerable flourish, threw down a second piece of a paper, etched in ink digits followed by an unforgivable number of zeroes, and declared, "And then here's the invoice for the wine." Stupified, I asked what the first figure was.

"The sh-e-e-ping, Monsieur. The sh-e-e-ping." I felt like bleating. I took the shipping invoice from him, and calmly and politely offered my excuses for not understanding the small fortune I would have parted with. Mr. Trintignant became cold-faced, except for the unmistakable signs of anger that shone in the redness of his ears. I tore the invoice up as, and murmured in embarrassment, that the sum was much too high, and should be saved for some catastrophic illness. "There's no free lunch, Monsieur."

"No, but there is a cheaper one next door. "

"Then do not waste my time." I went to a competitor across the street, bought a reasonably priced wine bottled at the damn chateau, and headed for the car. When I arrived I could hear the hymn, "God save the Queen," trailing from inside the car. I looked to see how the radio had been functioning without the ignition, and noticed the half-bottle of wine I had tucked on the floorboards to be uncorked and completely empty. Then I saw the green light flashing on the GPS, and discerned that the singing, which was significantly off key, was emanating from Henry's speaker. "Long live our noble queen, God shave the queen send her victorioush, happy..hic..and glorioush."

Mystified, I whispered, "Henry, you didn't."

"...scatter her enemies, and make them fall." He went on proudly, in what seemed like the original version of the Star Spangled Banner as sung in an aquarium. The only thing missing was a drunken bugler.

I did not realize the size of the issue until I had plugged in my next destination, which was Van Gogh's Arles.

Henry said at first, "Arles. Arles-sur-Merde?"

"Henry shut up! You know exactly what town I am referring to; the place where Vincent Van Gogh came to live."

"Van who?"

"Gogh."

"Where did Van go?"

"Where we are headed, you imbecile!" I thumbed through the Michelin guide in hopes I could navigate the trip by myself. Henry started again "..frushtrate their knavish tricksh, on her hopsh we fish,"

I spoke to myself, "South 120 kilometers."

In a final chorus, Henry blasted in his best baritone, "God Save the Queen."

"Arles, Henry. Come on!" I encouraged.

"Go backwards three hundred miles. In a figure eight." The voice had returned to its punctilious British accent.

Frustrated, I proceed down the autoroute and took the wrong turn at a turnabout, proceeding in the opposite direction of la Camargue, which was where Arles sat. I made a U-turn across the highway markers in a fit of anger. Henry was silent.

It was in a matter of seconds that I saw the red and blue lights of the gendarme's motorcycle behind me. I abruptly swerved to the shoulder. I rolled down the window as he stepped up to the door. A large belch emitted from the speaker of the GPS.

"Monsieur, vous venez de faire une maneuvre illegale."

Obviously, making a U-turn in mid-highway was illegal on this side of the Atlantic as well. I whooped he would just give me a ticket and have me move on. I handed my French passport to the officer, along with my California driver's license. He looked at me quizzically, and asked if I was American or French.

I said "Both, depending on..."

"...The nationality of the police officer," Henry retorted with a chuckle.

"Pardon?" Inquired the gendarme.

I said, "Rien,"which was, "nothing," which described what I wanted most to be at that precise moment. I pleaded my apologies, "Je suis navre, je pense que…"

"Vous avez la tete d'un cochon." Henry was apparently versed in completing sentences, particularly by telling the officer he had the head of a pig.

"Sortez de la voiture. Get out of ze car. Have you been drinking alcohol?"

This was going from bad to worse.

"No, Earl Grey, all the way." Henry replied. He repeated, "Earl Grey, all the way."

"This is not a joke!" The officer was becoming agitated.

I shrugged my shoulders. "I didn't say anything."

He told me to walk to his car so he could call another vehicle, purportedly to transport me to the local jail.

"Queue de poule," murmured from the car through the still open driver's door. Henry's musings had just referred to the gendarme as a chicken-butt.

The officer looked back in my rental car, as if searching for a second suspect.

"Je ne suis pas saoul!" I insisted firmly that I was not drunk, loudly trying to mimic what we had just heard. The officer scratched his head.

All at once, the radio on the police motorcycle blared. "Capitaine, laissez tombez. Accident fatale a l'intersection St. Emmanuel. Accident fatal a l'intersection, St. Emmanuel. Repondez, s'il vous plait." The gendarme, instantly communicated his understanding of the emergency call to the dispatcher and announced that he was on his way. He looked at me dismissively.

"Allez-vous en." Getting the hell out of dodge was a welcome request.

As I carefully drove down the highway at the required speed limit, Henry fell silent. We approached an intersection, which said St. Emmanuel. In the distance I saw a police motorcycle headed in one direction. There was neither any sign of traffic or vehicular mishap.

As I slowly drove on, Henry burped. And then I heard as the voice of the dispatcher played from the GPS, "Capitaine, accident fatale a l'intersection Emmanuel." Henry wasn't mimicking. He was inventing the voice. How he made it operate on the dispatcher's radio waves I will never know, anymore than I will understand how a GPS can get drunk off a bottle of wine.

As the sunset on the humid landscape of La Camargue, I brought the windows down, and Henry and I sang in unison together:
"It's a long way to Tipperary,
It's a long way to go.
It's a long way to Tipperary,
To the sweetest girl I know."

I woke up the next morning with a splitting hangover in my hotel room that bordered the area of the great arena of Arles. I had drunk a few forbidden Absinthes with a couple of backpackers at the Café de Nuit, memorialized in Van Gogh's great painting of the same name. My head, however, felt like the swirling skies of *A Starry Night*. Barely remembering the events of the day before, I limped to the site of the ancient Roman Baths, before touring the arena. The sun's rays beat on my brow, and I looked forward to arriving that evening in Carcassonne, the ancient fortified town in the Aude department built by Visigoths in the fifth century.

We never made it. On a deserted stretch of road the Avis rental-a-car's engine shut down and we coasted to a stop. Everything from the brakes to the power steering were in lock-down mode and even the battery barely held a glimmer of life. It was noon, and we were off the main road in search of the Canal du Midi, famous for its peaceful family rides on small river barges. The humidity hung in the air like a hot wave of steam. The mosquitoes were ravenous in the country stillness untrammeled by sounds of cars or people. I tried my cell-phone, but the people at its international headquarters couldn't even figure out what prefix I should dial to get a hold of the rental company in Nice. I looked at Henry, and the small glimmer of the green flashing light was flashing less and less. I walked around the car, wishing that I had at least stocked up on water and food. I felt extremely lonely. I kicked the car's tire and beat my fists on the hood. I assumed I could walk to a farmhouse, but wasn't even sure of which way to go. I was sure that if I picked the wrong one I would collapse from dehydration and days later my body would be found on the side of the road, swollen by bee stings and mosquito bites.

I got back in the car. In a slow voice that seemed to be on the wrong phonograph speed, Henry said: "Per...pi...gnan...train station." And then the voice sputtered.

"Henry, you there? Henry!" I assumed it was the battery but the strange thing was that the L.E.D. of the clock was still displaying the numbers of the hours and minutes.

After waiting ten more minutes for help that did not come, I took one last stab at starting the car. As I turned the key, the engine tuned over and coughed once. I got out of the car and saw that the car was on something of a downward slope. I unlatched the handbrake and pushed the car with all my weight as I ran holding the open driver's door. As the car gained a slow momentum, I jumped in and turned the ignition, the engine sputtered, once, and, then a second time, and the engine roared. For at least now we were in motion and going somewhere. The gauges showed that the engine was in the red zone so I traveled to back to the highway and followed the signs to Perpignan. I found the roundabouts and committed a number of errors in turns passing the train station at least six times. Henry's green light had stopped blinking, and his stentorian British accent was absent. I started humming, "God Save the Queen" as I watched the gauge for engine heat turn into the red zone while simultaneously watching the gas go straight to empty. Accidents come in threes and of course another warning was blinking. It was my bladder. I had exactly five minutes.

After trying vainly to follow the signs I turned down a blind alley and saw a set of railroad tracks and followed where they led. Ultimately, the train station of Perpignan with its clock tower and cafes appeared behind a set of tenements. I drove into a parking area, and with both hands grabbed for a kiosk parking ticket and my crotch simultaneously.

I looked to my right and saw the Avis sign like it was the second coming of Christ. I stopped the car, and the engine died for the last time. I raced to the counter and yelled, "Toilettes," as if I was screaming the word, "Fire," in a crowded theater. The man at the counter pointed to a non-descript door as if he had been directing traffic all his life. I slammed it shut and relieved myself as my biological clock hit the final second like the countdown of a bomb.

When I exited, the Avis people realized that the car's engine had failed on its own and supplied me with a replacement Peugeot. I moved my bags, glasses, and maps, and set my sights on Carcassonne. But then I realized that Henry was gone. I demanded my old GPS from the rental people, but they said my car had never been equipped with one. I told them that that was ridiculous and that I wanted my friend back. They looked at me like I had spent too much time in the sun. I took a minute, looked at the ground, and breathed deeply.

I got into the Peugeot and slowly drove out of the town of Perpignan. I had lost only two precious hours. I headed to Carcassonne, entering into the new town before turning left down a cobblestone street to the old ramparts. There they stood under the moonlight, magnificently bathed in the night lights that changed from red to blue to green, giving the fortified walls a certain Hollywood feel. I parked on the bridge and smelled the aromas of someone's roasting tournedos wafting through a kitchen window. The night air was cool along the river that circled the old town. I got back into the driver's seat and noticed a green light blinking. It was the GPS of the Peugeot. And then Henry's voice whispered, "I love you, Marc."

I smiled and responded, "Oh, Henry, you're just saying that."

The Case of the Red Walking Cane

Whatever Gene might say, I saw it *first*. Though he was the first to venture to the wooden canes poised against a wire fence at this open air market of African souvenirs, I was close behind, my eyes riveted to the array of tribal artifacts in search of that perfect Ndebele keepsake. No cheap woven baskets or ebony salad serving utensils for me. *I* was on a mission to find some large, solid, substantial object that was glorious enough for the mass adulation of dinner guests *and* eccentric enough to be light years away from the commercial Shona sculptures sold in L.A. stores; something big and heavy enough to underscore my travelers' perseverance in transporting a special but cumbersome artifact to the New World, some 6,000 miles away. I was the quintessential American tourist carting his souvenir trophy back from the safari hunt. As Gene fondled a more inferior and unstimulating stick of beech wood, probably used as a support cane for the less sophisticated tribes, my eyes locked on a walking cane one foot away that stood out like a diamond on a pile of rubble.

Made of deep red bubinga wood, carved in totem fashion with a warrior holding a spear atop an older man wearing a straw skirt, it set everything that needed to be said about African tradition, beautiful in its artistic simplicity, strong and supportive in its practical uses. I am one of those constantly frustrated shoppers, never quite satisfied with the first item that comes my way. I feel somehow that I have to work hours at it before parting with a dollar. Except on those rare occasions whereby a confluence of emergency, opportunism, and wild luck demand that I grab something immediately and yell, "Mine!" to the necessary exclusion of good friends that spot the rubble, but not the diamond first.

Which, in Zimbabwe, clearly was the case. Pouncing on the object, as I was nearest to it, I negotiated with the seller at length, never in doubt that I would purchase this bit of African culture no matter what the price. As Gene scoured the remaining sticks (and they were just sticks) for a second best, I even managed to get the merchant to throw in a traditional African zither to close the deal.proudly walking away with my prize, which cost perhaps eight American dollars. I stashed it in the conveniently horizontal tray of our Land Rover, usually left for storing binoculars and cameras, so that it would not chip or crack on the way back to the lodge. And I was home free.

Unfortunately, no amount of newspaper wrapping and masking tape quite brought that about. There was just one small problem. And it had less to do with 6,000 miles of rental car and air transport than it did with a certain synaptic lapse in my brain that tends to occur when transporting objects of value. Like the time on the eve of trial as a prosecuting attorney that I had left all of the People's evidence on a murder case in the trunk of a rental car that I had returned the night before—including the weapon used, a hatchet. But that's another story.

Perpetually afflicted by absentmindedness, I had already left one sweatshirt in Plettenberg, South Africa that I had to have couriered to Jo'burg for twice the value of the shirt. But what can replace sentimental attachment? Surely, not money. Even though with this last relapse of Alzeimhers' I was about to put DHL on the map in Southern Africa. So what? And okay, perhaps I was a little too profligate in my purchases of Shona artifacts at that marketplace in Bulawayo. Deluged by kids coming at you like the worst strain of used car salesmen, it's easier to purchase an item from the pursuing throng and get it over with than to mercilessly ignore them as if they did not exist so that you can march in a straight line like a horse wearing blinders. And the little Lolita of Bulawayo with all her tugging and pulling and begging needed a few bucks to eat lunch, even though by that time it was 6:00 in the evening . I had already paid for three lunches and gotten one soon-to-be broken Hippo sculpture in return. But then I should never have left it in the back trunk of the rental while doing the Cannonball run through the Matopos Game Park. If my friend Karl had just escorted her to the supermarket then, I wouldn't have this fixation with hippos. But next to the red walking cane, that obsession paled in comparison. At least I bought a straw basket with which to carry all those souvenirs. As for the cane, I should have impaled myself with it. That way there was some certainty it might have made it home.

At the age of thirty five memory is not what it used to be, and after painstakingly packing and taping my cane, I left it in the corner of our seedy hotel room in the Holiday Inn in Bulawayo, Zimbabwe, where it must've been fairly lonely for some time. I've now persuaded myself that the newspaper clipping wrapped carefully around this stick must have been camouflaged so well by the yellowed walls of this under-renovation hovel, to put it lightly, that it completely missed my attention, if not that of Housekeeping.

So there I was. Driving the rental back to Huange National Airport when I smacked myself in the forehead, and for the first time realized that I had left my prized walking stick, the culmination of four weeks of browsing through street side markets, the steal of all time, leaning invisibly in the corner of a hotel room 300 miles behind.

It is one thing to have done it once or twice in your lifetime, like the time you took a nap and awoke an hour later in the daylight thinking you had slept through the next day of work, then dressed in a suit and went to work 14 hours early. Or maybe the time your father took you on the sailboat when you were seven and asked for the jib line and you handed him the chord from your windbreaker. There were always enough stories around the family table about my pathological absentmindedness. This state of affairs is tougher to deal with alone for it is then that you become your worst critic. And when these transgressions are so common, they become a fact of life. They say that a blind person enhances his other senses out of necessity. I compensated for my short attention span by having fine-tuned fall-back positions:

three spare sets of keys, two alarm clocks, and drawn curtains to shock the sun into my sleepy body to be punctual at work, an endless stream of post-it notes on walls to remind me of events (birthdays, my graduation), and a lifetime membership in Triple AAA.

But there was no fail-safe for my red walking cane, precious objet d'art, left to be scavenged by the sordid thievery of the next night's hotel tenants that would take hold of it and sell it on the black market.

I must have been sick to my stomach. On the way to catch our flight, which was another crucial link-up in our itinerary and for which we were running just a bit late, we passed once again by the same marketplace where I had bought the cane and I insisted in no uncertain terms that we stop so that I could find another $8.00 replacement. The car's engine was still on. The guys watched nervously, lest I become embroiled in another lengthy consumer haggling spree at the expense of our flight. I was very good. But I did not find another cane. They had not renovated the pile of rubble. So I returned with a $10.00 drum. I thought this might provide me with some solace and that my aching for the perfect souvenir would be satiated.

Not to be. It was a cheap good-for-nothing drum with a parched wildebeest skin and little cheesy dowels through the front rim that made the drum resound with a sullen "boom, boom, boom." And though it was priced at a reasonable 40 zimbabwe dollars, it would've been preferable had they not engraved the price in blue ink on the side of the drum for all to see. I don't recall ever admiring a valuable antiquity in someone's home, from some other era or culture, embossed with a price tag translated into the current exchange rate. The drum clearly did not have the dignity of my walking cane.

At the airport we waited two and a half hours for our departure, plenty of time to have gone back to get the cane. While publishing our problems in the daily airlinecomplaint album that was now five inches thick, I proceeded to make a number of calls to DHL, that famous 'can do' courier service, luckily with an office in Bulawayo, from an outside airport phone.

This phone was located on the outside grounds of the airport on the other side of the customs anteroom, which of course required a special agreement with the customs officer. *Please don't strip search me every time I run back to see if the plane has arrived. Please provide me with change for the phone, as I will apparently need more than a single human being can carry between trips. Please provide me with the phone number of a courier company that doesn't put me on hold and then gets disconnected every time I call. Please provide me with a napkin so that I might clean out the corpses of mosquitoes that keep clogging the coin slot on the public phone. Please give me a drink.*

One would think a courier company was schooled in the business of dealing with distressed customers making urgent sweaty phone calls from public airports. This is where their market lies. The incompetent and procrastinating public, who failed to take advantage of the slower mainstream postal services with sufficient lead-time, who failed to learn how to recycle their old cardboard boxes and grocery bags into postal parcels brimming with gifts and an inexpensive strip of stamps. *No, we don't need delivery in one week or three days, or by boat, air, or the pony express. We need it tomorrow, now, or yesterday; in the case of birthdays, one week ago.* Or in my case, now at the airport in Huange, Zimbabwe, tonight at the Holiday Inn in Johannesburg, South Africa; tomorrow at Sun City; and in three days in Torrance, or Manhattan Beach, California, depending on if I go to work.

I spoke in very slow monosyllables on the public phone while mosquitoes crawled into the receiver: C-A-L-I-F-O-R-N-I-A

Ever heard of it? It's in the United States of America. Home of Hollywood, beaches, Baywatch, and that soap opera, *Santa Barbara* whose reruns you are all watching. Still don't get it? Alright, let's start with the word *capitalism*. The people at the Bulawayo Holiday Inn, bless their hearts, were having the most basic difficulty merely interfacing with the diction of this panicked American, who was I dare say growing uglier by the minute. Ever conscious of my penchant for swallowing entire syllables, I tried my best British Colonial and was encouraged when Holiday Inn Housekeeping finally understood that I was seeking a tribal artifact, and not a pair of crutches. But I had run out of change before I could tell them where in the room I had left it . . .

My search then became a twelve-step program that began at a phone booth covered with mosquitoes outside of an airport waiting to board a plane at any moment. Step one could be divided into four substeps. First, I must describe the item. Second, I must explain where I left it so that they may take immediate possession of it. Third, they must physically send it to me. Fourth, I must be where they send it. By the time I boarded our much-delayed Zimbabwe airlines flight two hours later I had completed step one.

When the plane left the tarmac, I had put out a desperate message into the African universe wondering how in the world a poorly run Holiday Inn could understand—not to mention afford—to to package and send a walking cane without so much as a credit card to bill it to.

The other fear was that I might receive some crippled persons crutches instead.

I arrived home safely but exhausted from my African adventure. Life resumed. Months went by in the Torrance office. Cases were tried. One day, two boxes arrived which I was expecting – filled with souvenirs: two bottles of Stellenbosch wine, two figurines of an old man leaning on – yes, a walking cane - a carving of a parade of elephants and a water buffalo, a pouch of hot Indian curry powder, salad servers made out of ibex horns, a couple of sarongs and some smelly underwear. I really hate when people at work, in a fluster of excitement, poke around in your newly arrived box of African loot only to first uncover a pair of smelly sweat socks that had hiked the veld of Huange National Park.

The overpowering smell of the curry was my saving grace. It masked the other odors effectively. But still no walking cane.

One day a package arrived in a long box that was folded upon itself, both ends hanging together by a strip of packing tape. I curiously examined the parcel and saw some reddish wood sticking out of a hole in the postal wrapping. It was my stick, or my two half sticks, I should say. It was as if the DHL courier had examined the cane and decided that it was more cost-efficient to break it into two pieces on his knee before sending it.

I was crestfallen.

Looking at this pair of twin carvings each displaying a jagged broken edge, I was however comforted by the fact that the walking cane, even in pieces, had made it six thousand miles to my office desk in Southern California. I went home and noticed that the broken edges, with their protruding shards, still could fit together and complete the whole. I glued the two pieces together and propped the stick against the wall.

The next morning I found the two pieces lying next to each other on the carpet. The glue had not stuck. I felt that some African demon had infused itself in the bubinga wood and had come to visit the ravages of ironic disappointment upon me.

In a taunting voice, the demon spoke. "Here. Take your stick, you vulgar tourist, and I will haunt your shopping sprees for the rest of your days."

Surprised at this voice, I shakily retorted, "I was merely trying to bring home a token of your beautiful country so I could be reminded of it in my daily urban grind. Besides, I have just the spot for it on a narrow length of wall."

Not missing a beat, the demon replied, "Who are you to believe you can import our culture like a product and hang it up above your mantelpiece to boast of your whirlwind international travels?"

To which I exclaimed, "But it would look so cool right there," pointing to a blank wall in the foyer. "Somewhere between the Peruvian plate and the faux seventies terrarium under the tiled stairs. I promise to pay my respects to it every morning." The terrarium needed décor; the plants had all but died, except the plastic ones, and even they were wilting.

The spirit angrily exclaimed, "I should do the same thing with your head, preferably shrunken to a more appropriate size, and place it on a tree outside of my makeshift hut, as we are rapidly running out of interior space for decorating purposes."

Finding myself standing in the middle of my living room talking to a piece of broken wood, I walked out of the apartment and around the block.

I returned shortly, and not persuaded by the spirit of Artifacts Passed, I glued the two pieces of the cane back together again, hoping that they would finally stick, and I drove to work.

I returned home that day and I was amazed. The stick had stayed together. I wired a loop and hung it on the wall. And it hung there in the foyer for two years until it became one of the centerpieces of the living room of my new home, where it now hangs between two windows that look out onto the birds of paradise and verbenia of my flower bed that greets visitors as they approach the front porch. The red walking cane takes its place among many things I have taken home from travels, some with an equally unique story to tell: an Ottoman Empire coffee grinder, a Moroccan vase, a Thai guitar, an Iguaçu flechette and bow.

I remembered how the market salesman had explained that the cane was representative of Ndebele life: the young warrior holding his spear, standing on the head of the elderly wise man, who stood on a curved handle. But these souvenirs do not serve to bring this culture, this warrior, this wise man, to the United States. They are only small remembrances that infuse my life with the memories of travels to another world. A world of raw senses, of poverty, of cultures that are simple yet visceral. I look at framed photographs every day of places I have been that remind me occasionally that I have seen for one small moment a great deal of the world, and that my house for all its décor is a house of many places.

I place even the shells and stones I religiously collect from the trails and beaches of foreign countries into obscure stone boxes and dense garden planters, with the thought of importing the karma of other civilizations to bless my home with good fortune. Thus, in that corner are those green stones from a beach in Italy, here is a rock from the Incan Trail, and there is a shell from Tierra del Fuego. If they are even noticed by houseguests, they are merely acknowledged as aesthetically pleasing rocks of the earth. But for me they mean so much more.

As for the demon, he never returned. I imagine he had bigger fish to fry.

The Book

Gone. Jeff Sanders scanned the shelf at the Jester Center cafeteria and the damn book was nowhere to be seen. Gone. Disappeared. Stolen. Stolen from the 'safe' counter where students checked their school backpacks before eating their share of mess hall slop of pizza and the current version of Salisbury steak, complete with a helping of overcooked squash. Who would steal a chemistry book at the height of finals, especially when the student was within feet of viewing the incident probably with his teeth sunk in a corn on the cob that had been boiled much too long? Jeff Sanders was distressed. The book, like all university textbooks, was an overpriced tome that comprised one of the central aspects of tuition. It was about the evils of global warming and the composition of the toxic chemicals produced by coal firing plants, and Jeff Sanders absolutely needed it to study for his final that was in three days. He had psyched himself to memorize every last chemical equation, every last public policy statement regarding the pressing subject of public health, and every aspect of plant biology that he could mentally ingest, but he needed the damn book, and it was now gone. It cost $35.99 at the local university co-op and he had $15.41 in his checking account. Jeff had prepared himself for the ultimate cram session of the fall semester, legal pad and pen ready to copiously outline the chapters of the book. It was the book of the class whose lectures he had slept through, the book he intended to read from front to back for the next two nights, with a little sleep in between and the help of some no-dose purchased at the university pharmacy. *No book* spelled an "F."

His parents had always taught him to never lose sight of his belongings and he had been diligent about locking his dorm room door, developing trust in the right people, like his resident assistant who had just recently had a talk with him about his grades, as he had been observed pulling all-nighters, not because of freshman college study but due to chasing young co-eds all across campus. Though Jeff Sanders made A's, he made them by the seat of his pants. He still, however, protected what was his and usually labeled every last possession, his name glowing in yellow highlighter even on his toiletry case.

Jeff Sanders thought about his predicament. No money to buy a book, no one else to borrow it from. No book, and he would fail the class. There had to be some other solution. He could go and give plasma to make a few bucks, but he didn't have the time to be sitting on a hospital bed donating his fluids when he needed to be reading about the hazards of asbestos. He needed the book. Now.

Jeff Sanders knew the book was still for sale at the usual price at the Co-op. He didn't have the money to buy it, or even a credit card to his name. He thought and finally convinced himself that he had to steal one. He was a victim of theft, and he now was going to respond in kind. He felt some comfort in knowing that a cooperative university bookstore was like a corporation anywhere; they could better absorb the loss of a theft of one book than one poor student who desperately needed his education.

Jeff Sanders tested the fall weather and felt that it was cold enough in the early morning to wear a long trench coat. He stuck an algebra book in his belt, riding on the back of his pants, and donned the trench coat and began to walk in his 15 by 8 foot dorm room like a young person afflicted with spina bifida. This way the book would not stick out through his coat like a big flag that alerted security that a book, a large one, was not checking in at the cashier's line before leaving the store. The exercise seemed to work, but then the weather in Texas changes. If you are wearing a trench coat in Texas, it better be damned cold. Otherwise, make sure to wear something underneath. And wearing a trench coat in your freshman year of college at high noon did not exactly make a fashion statement.

Jeff Sanders walked up Guadalupe Street in Austin headed towards the bookstore. It was known as the Drag, though it had been years since students had sped their old Chevy's with their tires squealing down this strip of road that bordered the campus. There was one hamburger stand, a spate of clothing shops, an old theatre, and the odd tattoo parlor and dive that gave the street its bohemian character. Other than that, it was student housing, college unions, and supply stores that masked the opulent fraternities and sororities that started one street across. There was the ubiquitous homeless woman, Hail Mary, who verbally assaulted the passersby with her fire and brimstone speeches, warning all sinners that they would soon die in the fires of Hell. Most people snickered and silently imitated the way she pronounced, "F-i-i-i-re," but only after they had cleared her presence by walking another block. Jeff wondered what choice epithet she would yell at him for harboring the intent to steal a book from the University Co-op, that sacred cow. He imagined that she would relegate him to the dark bowels of Hades where people were lashed with a leather whip while a large deformed falcon pecked away at their eyes. Wearing his trench coat, he sauntered into the bookstore bent over like the hunchback of Notre Dame. If it was necessary to conceal the stolen book from suspicion, it was also necessary to consistently display this manufactured handicap. Jeff wasn't sure if video cameras were used in the store to catch shoplifters, but he wasn't going to take any chances.

He walked to the basement where the schoolbooks were stacked high in rows that made you feel like you were walking through a miniature city of skyscrapers constructed out of countless sets of shiny hardbound books towering over the aisles of graphic drawing pencils, three punch binders, and art class easels. He walked over to the chemistry section, but only after noting a storage room at the end of the aisle where books were stocked and waiting to be put on display. Finally, he saw the pile of Chemistry 101 Books at the corner next to volumes of Organic Chemistry. He consoled himself with the fact that his chemistry class was not the career busting monster course that Organic Chemistry was reputed to be. No matter, he still desperately needed that book. He plucked one off the top of the pile and examined it quickly, feigning interest in its subject matter.

Quietly, he made his way to the storeroom and closed the door behind him. He removed his overcoat. The book was square and heavy, but he was able to cinch it in the belt at the back of his pants. He had to bend slightly forward to keep it from jutting out like a broken vertebrae. He donned the trench coat, which completely covered up his backside, and peering though the door's square window, he quickly walked back into the aisle when it was empty of shoppers. Limping along like some unfortunate accident victim, he cleared the turnstile and walked past the cashier, shaking his head in disappointment as if he was crestfallen not to have found the item he was looking for.

Holding the small of his back, he made it to the front entrance, his eyes furtively moving from side to side to ascertain that some loss prevention officer hadn't spied his crime. Outside, the sun's rays hit him squarely in the eyes, even if it was just slightly cold enough to wear a trench coat. Jeff surveyed the Drag for security guards that often sat outside in unmarked cars waiting to pounce on the shoplifters who emerged from stores with merchandise concealed on their persons. Jeff stepped away from the entrance and began walking down the sidewalk, still parading as a hunchback, the stolen book secured in his waistband.

He wasn't expecting Hail Mary. She stood at the entrance of an alley like a sentinel, her eyes scanning the parade of sinners that walked before her.

She yelled at Jeff, "You are a heathen, Mister." He tried to look like she must be addressing some other unlucky customer. But she was unrelenting. "Don't you ignore me, you Judah. Ye will burn in the fires of hell for having drunk the wine of Sat-a-a-a-a-n!"

Before he knew it, bent over with trench coat on, she had stepped directly in front of him, raging at him like the Wrath of God embodied in a waif-like avenging angel, wearing a dirty white cotton dress sporting a bible in one hand and a accusing finger in the other, which was now pointing at him with her arm outstretched as if he were the newly discovered Anti-Christ. People began to gather as if it was a Sunday hanging. Jeff was left standing there, his passage obstructed, his back painfully bent to avoid detection of the chemistry book tucked in the seat of his pants.

"Ye are the demon that shall never walk through the gates of heaven. Ye are the swine that has cast away the love of God, for the love of e-v-i-i-l-l-l!"

Jeff Sanders looked nervously about. He could not maintain his stance much longer in his hunched position. Not a block from the Co-op, he was an eyesore on the sidewalk, no less than Hail Mary.

He retorted, "Get away from me, you bitch," which only got the crowd laughing more.

Like a chorus, she yelled back, "Ye have lied down with snakes, and have become one." All he could think about was wishing he was one. That way he could bite her with his poisonous fangs and watch her writhe on the sidewalk. But he kept his composure.

He knelt in front of her and with every ounce of control he could muster; he let his head down and muttered loud enough for all to hear, "I have sinned. I repent. Forgive my sins, as you forgive those who have sinned against you. I am a vile, untrustworthy snake that has seen the ill of his ways. I want to come home!"

Without flinching, Mary touched his shoulder and softly said: "You are the child of God. You will be forgiven. Repent your sins and ye shall be forgiven and led unto the house of God."

Exasperated, Jeff yelled out almost in derision, as if he was playing along with the crowd, "I do. I do. I am a bad man. I have done evil. I throw myself upon the mercy of God, and I repent my sins!"

Right when a sly smile was about to crack his face, he felt the book plop out of his pants and onto the pavement like a loud clap. He was mortified. The spectators now switched their attention to the glistening new chemistry book that had emerged from the person of the accused and had fallen onto the pavement like a smoking gun. A man dressed in blue khakis and a white button down shirt approached Jeff, who was kneeling frozen on the sidewalk.

The man exclaimed, "Hey. That's a Co-op book. You were hiding it. Where's your bag?" Jeff looked quizzically at him. He wondered if maybe he should have just brought an empty Co-op shopping bag into the store, placed the book in it, and walked out like a normal person without all this trench coat fanfare. Jeff shrugged his shoulders. The man continued, "Well hell, son, you better have a receipt!" Jeff could see where this was going. The crowd had now doubled and Hail Mary stood silently, her eyes like black saucers, fuming with indignation at Jeff Sanders, who didn't know what to say. There it was, that beautiful hardbound second edition of *The World in Chemistry; the Building Blocks of Life*, the road to his passing his final exam, laying on a dirty sidewalk off the Drag, in front of a crowd of onlookers, and about to be repossessed by its rightful owner.

Jeff knew enough about criminal law not to admit a thing. "I do not know what you are talking about, Sir."

But the man responded by taking hold of Jeff and saying "Oh, I think you do, young man. You have stolen that book, haven't you?"

Jeff replied, "I didn't steal a thing, asshole!"

The security guard lifted him physically off the pavement and began to escort him to the front of the store. Jeff resisted. "I am not going anywhere." The last thing he needed was an encounter with the law to seal his educational fate for good. The man stopped, began to take out a pair of handcuffs, and asked for Jeff's identification. Jeff pulled out his wallet and showed the man his drivers' license, which the man scribbled on a piece of paper. "Your name is Jeff Sanders?" Jeff nodded.

The man reached for the book that still lay on the sidewalk, but all of a sudden Hail Mary, who had been repeating, "Vengeance sayeth the Lord" like a mantra, kicked the book away from him.

He looked at her in shock and exclaimed, "Mary, what are you doing? We have talked about this." The book slid off the curb, and the front cover opened.

Mary, as if transformed, declared, "He has repented! He has been saved. He is the chosen one!"

The guard, trying to retrieve the book, commanded, "Woman, get back!"

She responded, in a voice pregnant with premonition, "Thou shalt obey the rule of God, or thou shalt suffer his wrath!"

About to retrieve the open book from the sewer, the guard stopped and looked questioningly at it. He looked over at Jeff. "What did you say your name was?"

Jeff muttered under his breath, "Jeff Sanders."

The guard picked up the book and approached Jeff standing in handcuffs, still wearing his trench coat in front of the crowd. With his key, he unlocked them. Gruffly, the guard said to Jeff, "Get out of here." He picked up the book and handed it to Jeff. The crowd was astonished. Murmurs ran across their lips like silent whispers.

Mary stood in front, now playing the role of Joan of Arc. "Ye have been forgiven by the Almighty. Ye shall change your ways and work for the good of God. Clean thyself of the sins of Satan, and be free."

Jeff Sanders got up off the ground, took off his trench coat and without saying a word, took the book in hand, straightened out his back and started walking back to the campus. When he got to the dormitory and made his way to his room he set the book down on a desk and took a deep breath. Beads of sweat ran down his forehead. He thought to himself, "Oh, Jeff Sanders, that was another close call." He could not imagine what a theft conviction would have done to his career. Not to mention what his parents would think. As penance, he thought it would be sufficiently punishing to begin studying the first chapter of the book for his final.

He opened the book, and was surprised by the first thing that he saw. The name "Jeff Sanders" was displayed in the inside cover of the chemistry book. It stood there in block letters printed in yellow highlighter, with Jeff's dorm room number appearing underneath. His parents had taught him well.

When books were stolen, they were often sold back to the original store for a percentage of the price. While Jeff was splitting his sides laughing on his dormitory floor something deep inside of him lightened its weight, donned wings and flew away. The doors of Heaven were still open for him. The book was his.